Give Forest
Its Next Portent

Also by Peter Larkin

Enclosures
Prose Woods
Pastoral Advert
Terrain Seed Scarcity
Slights Agreeing Trees
Sprout Near Severing Close
Rings Resting The Circuit
What the Surfaces Enclave of Wang Wei
Leaves of Field
Lessways Least Scarce Among
Imparkments (The Surrogate Has Settled)

Wordsworth and Coleridge: Promising Losses

PETER LARKIN

Give Forest Its Next Portent

Shearsman Books

First published in the United Kingdom in 2014 by
Shearsman Books
50 Westons Hill Drive
Emersons Green
BRISTOL
BS16 7DF

Shearsman Books Ltd Registered Office
30–31 St. James Place, Mangotsfield, Bristol BS16 9JB
(this address not for correspondence)

www.shearsman.com

ISBN 978-1-84861-384-3

Acknowledgements

I am grateful to the following magazines and their editors where extracts from some of these texts first appeared:

Blackbox Manifold, Cordite, Free Verse, LQR, No Prizes, Plumwood Mountain, Shearsman, Stride, Snow, Tears in the Fence, UnAmerican Activities, Yellowfield.

An extract from 'Brushwood by Inflection' first appeared in my *Wordsworth and Coleridge: Promising Losses* (New York: Palgrave, 2012).

It's a pleasure to thank these individuals for support, advice and friendship: Anthony Barnett, Ian Brinton, Amy Cutler, Mark Dickinson, Matthew Hall, Edmund Hardy, Ian Heames, Michael Heller, Louise Ho, Emma Mason, Anthony Mellors, Edric Mesmer, Sophie Seita, Jonathan Skinner, G.C. Waldrep, Tom West.
My especial gratitude to Tony Frazer for publishing a third collection of my work in his splendid press.

Contents

BRUSHWOOD BY INFLECTION

2010

The less of life remains, the more seductive it is for consciousness to take the bare harsh remnants of the living for the appearance of the Absolute.

Theodor Adorno

Les branches sont libres de n'avoir pas de fruits.

René Char

For if they do this when the wood is green, what will happen when it is dry?

Luke 23.31

A minor break dis-alienating for the purpose of a meta-embrace

Mark Dickinson

Note

The "inflection point" on a branch is where the direction of curve outwards changes to the direction of curve upwards, and is usually a play-off between elastic bending and thickening growth. A branch bends continuously even while it thickens and as such the shape of a branch can be seen as a function of time. But any break-off from that branch provokes a compunction of space across a strewnness which wrangles with its proneness before horizon.

So "inflection" in these texts has a more speculative association, not so much with permanent deformation, as with the trails of brushwood matting which surround trees or edge out beyond their line. After the break from main branch comes a further twist towards these given-aways' own sensory of gift amid a heaping-up of separation. Now tree becomes the agent for which branch appears the source and brush is the locus.

1

Given brushwood isn't code for a wrenched thing lying across
origin but the inflection of it is   forescatter where the young
of the year are broken in advance of the trees' own persistence
—a cob of green cud spat out by the trees's specialism to vacate
shoulder but recast the forks of surface   extending bent matter
to the neck of horizon

where roots creep to their edge quota, brush has swept past bed
to lie out on jammed marginal rota

any scattering of timber ends in this break perfectly ramified:
nothing pans out unless along what little of itself could sift
within the collapse-complexion

with breach off-tree
even more world-weight
crutched on sur-
face to margin

For brushwood doubt is not the crackle of itself but what flicker
there is in such brittle abandonment's spite of intricate granting
—a girdling gives meta-closure, or more openly inflects what
brash has bristled from mesh   the fibre of distribution no
longer a hollow of the intervals themselves

push from forest
to brushwood,
horizontal graze
bunchwards

Where brushwood trips at faltered roots to re-abrupt them, fold
in juxtaposition what is the brittle turn to origin ahead of fuelled
despairs mimicking fluent repairs

laid over beds of reliance, reaching for the hatchings' more
shareable (castable) compliance   inflected gamut of a terseness

earlier than alien, rough intractives on a planet surge to brushwood

where adjacent segments of tree meet their inflection points, their bitter parts waving out the scatter at an horizonal confluence

infinite seriality
lopped rigid
in devotion to a
singled inflect-
ion of gift
traceway through
brushwood beat
of the tread

These deferred tree-limbs inspect the path, smaller resuscitants in degree of drop   with the bind of inflection stay ceased throughout the straying: a spray of unbudded but deep-seated co-emption bare with deserved array towards the horizon's plain

in binding the evolute of a curve to the given, crossed by the perched sticks of separation   respects slightness in any replete defeated choice, the bend itself reseated

what can be screened from floor to be granted at the snick of a broken finger which a detached hand gets to fan out   reattaches at full extent only as this joint circumvents its precise severance part

glisters in inflected
quiet of woods
after the break
with crash

the outmapped
lay nestling
in the inflicted

Any exhausted root thin to be codified (re-shed): inflectional stratum wrinkles retrenchment slung post-extant   pales of brush no longer billeted on earth shornface but go counter-depleting where cannot be *inversely* lopped, *ie* regress to parent stem would be capped at longest offspring weald across the grain of origin

brushwood lacks its own climate envelope, apart from inflection never strains for a saturation by horizon in bunch   depletion remains the very sparsity schedule of outreach

benched within the disparate affix-risk of gift, connections not ill-torn but embossed on fallen place to last out (as first fallers) the vertical tides they are tossed from

sword of brush under
broad curve, cure of
branch offset by
cut to branch

The vine round the knotted root sketches a brushwood of outcome, at the dishevelment of origin, pushed over penetrable core at the strike off sapling   springy brush laid out to the wire, jutted breast of the depredation   such slights are parallel in heap laid out of, weathers of the not were corrosive enough for no veering *more* than origin

a forest of poor relations but in brushwood stamp of crabby retention: buffer the encroach of a nakedness unable to crouch enough   as trunk is to branch so brush is to the contra-fill off aperture, as goes with it stored wary to horizon

tempestible, splinter-
towering, most impassable
but *at* a shoulder
of smeared clearing
as wedge cast from root
cages margins of the un-
vacancy to within de-
grees of lashwood

Avenues of the dislocation projectively harbour their cross-
over, its strewnness a sharper stare than neutral severance alone,
scarcer at spread than living the staple to root   horizon winded
on this faggot hillock aspires no second wound

each angle out of hold now pervious accelerative lattice, the
estrangement hollow with after-tangle of inflective array   fed
to a bundle minus compression, detaches from root but awarded
the creep-margin that relies on dis-upright   the chips anti-
rotate off rendered trees or stand in for a cheaper scurf of the
ramification

dissipative reduct-
ion let substrate-
refill be for
brushwood export

Thickly laid over with a new scarcity's post-quickness as at any
finding mean of overgrowth   this bides the eventual scene of
hold   traps exuding brushwood until let go again as the tree of
it, dries out a ceiling to the tips   a debris of requital protrudes
from frame and puts the rap on horizon

rest the decrease poaching brushwood for tracking what re-
accustom it rakes to the least   fringe at horizon's edge raggedly
severed into lurch of pretext, forward repose leans long into
new taperings of dependence: a good-enough soil made scanty
ventricle where a mesh-haul of intersecting sticks sucks the pump

limbed for its
barebounds, the tree's
closely unsprained
fine losings,
indurable sphere
stepped to lending

A brushwood thicket lashed to the open, not taken aback once
out of hiding but braced separably for inflection   cut universally

falls to local devices, the scatter is neat horizon parabolic severed from tube just what intact ramification can't disuse for cleaving post-jointed by the primary detour of mercy

left packed at site unelbowing until it comes to relay severed joints on junctionless surfaces incommensurate sweep-over tailed by horizon, reproved for terrain but not removed from recoil, the detraction undespoiled in just such a carve across swerve

cover the cleared area while shipping brush off deserted trees, anchorless in vessel to connect the sag in capsized root

scrunted but slouchless
no scrub brushwood but
rubs out from high tree

backwardly out to
hollow wrist, each eye-
let unmists the gap
between branch-querk

Ungraded divergence one sole series thing far off at nearest severance to horizon taskable surface ventilates an architectonic of trees in belt as if they couldn't be paltry enough to thread their belongings on the lateral

as the obstruct is (a gift at hand) to the claw of torn from root

dark wood's shortcut to a comparison of ground now such obstacles inflecting less sorely over the same split unseamed, it hushes beyond the crash of it but doesn't silence the litter

the part played by trees in separatives of integral way: slighting the scattered chink means stitches mis-sweeping repart the open as at any treeless place, exactitude in ex-branch no longer severely spindling the ground

the crack into one
another's inflected
postfix of arrival

primed clear of its
rammed facets, what
the ramific spares

Time in joints dejects weak numbers until frailed in brushwood, the whole is claimant about dismembering, a disjunction thrown on the lay-it-from with time for assarts   of a world seen from across real extra-inherence on this rootless spur of flightlessness

extent of displacement serves as nearness index for the commoning brushed into, dry reeds of horizon: this feature detaches extent but not an outbed bent forwards of the exposure: brushwood is source splay even before its own torso-replay

among the abraded
verticals, what gives
horizon its saltings
arid stir of root
the untying tries for a
woundless vent in horizon

Inflect this second element in surprise horizon: the filigree catastrophe lies wadged before a non-collider beckoning the sprigs of origin   blaze off that fork minus handle at its unscorched scar across, bare particulars of forward radiant desertion whose highlights cluster in dissimmersion

unspasmic élan, the leap there is in ramification bridging itself for severed   a shiver darting at horizon's congestion concessionally arrived   brusque new mapping in circuit sashes, the lattice of main-tree bereaves field across the lace of nearest dependent shedding

brushwood a new door
to old branches
beaten at the threshold

resurges horizon
at once abjection
off tree filament

Grazing barrenness over ruck yet to be closely scarred this way, dropping fineals pluck a disconnection ample enough to be as pliant before the scratch of origin

our vanguard thrusting itself no further fear than open spires of landing outside the height

strike longwards toss,
bend tip abroad of
the lacks of approach

Precept learnt at a yard of waste brushed by unexpended tips against hard horizon   the crushing had already taken place at the gift from root: drift never supinely subsequent once taken *for* inflection: the sense in which brushwood cast is more internal to trees than own lame root

no mean inlay, how same-side tree radial went out to recombine without distributing its access more hollowly than: awaiting a bind at outspread itself

this divestment is openness throughout quanta of the given-to by adhesion in site of dropdown   comes to ramified flesh what can no longer be found amid vein of tree, new porches elapse to grazing the zone before horizon

cathected from tree
do it well to inflect
harrassed flailings
of gift

lost from the bays of
tree but won for
exploded graft
before origin

2

No longer such latency but pure encroaching congregation—
brushwood escapade at risk of a tree's owing longest the touch of
itself, in quest of what it has cast beyond grown attenuation—
the trees' retractile debris unsown forward, at rest on bestowing
the givens' encumber to ground

surrenderable component, leakage of tree onto a dry gutter of
inflection, clatter of origin on the heath crabbed with fingering
the reliances of debris

slippage snap its wattles at a vane of inflection around bouts of
outer keeping   condenses a rattled slightness upon ground, in
this despite tentacular for horizon

transmast accosts
severance that roots
counter-cross
reverence

Tree fragments decapped to their ulterior tips, tipping onto
hindrance allays heedless ground   this non-delay won't back-
joint against any offer of adoption among the strewns

grist take peripheries as apprised, scarce figure of branch-window
across what excess the tree embrasure will put to gap, separates
become its narrowing zone only in the ratio of a fore-plenty
hipped over

broken open a long way next to, according novel packets of fret,
a lately congruous outside imbricates acrid rim   scatter towards
foyer of horizon beyond what shells of limbs remain shelved in
tall forest

distended pivots
wildly reportive of
loosened gantry

spread gentle crane
on horizon

Dis-attempted flakes forwards, the achieved welter is counter-recessive though pawned on horizon   a rekeying from a layer of crisp contamination laying out lowest resource on, horizon trimmed by the oblique wrong of it   statics of rim, narrates frame of ground to touch from its own veridical off-trim by tree

a spray of inflection sheafing what is bent to edge lank and wide before the shelter it predicts   sheer flutter in the feral knees gone slender: naked periphery an earth now rakeable to ramified crustal zest

limbs in respoke across
fens of shards wherewithal
they plait debased

a spirelet sips
poor sapling
reversions of hold,
a fascine-bundle
shall well the batches
dilating from turn

Broken not shunted and so bequeathed to inflection   a bristle expelled from shaft towards unsnaring pending   what is no longer suspended but grounded hangs terrain over horizons of the slump, gashed heaviest in free external spoke   a brush of tidal inflection is interwoven flimsily beside the weirs of horizon: high tracts outbreathing their bare signs of alignment

though the cut was unique, brushwork will never singularise in branch because of it: the entire array staffs aspread at fall

damage had its own stolen impulse, renovation given in less-than towards what inflects against a wound's identical indication:

the random circulation of traumatic closures can't have been squandered on the same elation

micro-amended
sentience at a
porch's tree-low
prolapse entry

From brow over root under the scabless chin of horizon where brushwood shunts sacking to the imperative rim   soothed on the flush, desertion thickens to enflangement, whose insertibles do get branded abroad by a brushwood in steep exilic remission

brush where its starter tree is no taller than rising bracken   how a broken cleaves to place without a vertical wafer of repleteness— small leak of timbers but hems them quilting the thrash

brushwood given matrix within which any other times than sutured on horizon amid its recursion will have been snapped

the trees push out
horizon unchipped
but gathered apart

branched aftermath
of today's
broken stalk

Staled fernwork not much congealing but hauled under horizon by its unsalience   a quandary sown towards, creamed from, chiasmic lattice intricate at its ground delivery

distends through each lozenge of slightness where any in-reach-of is allowed to break the round, from now on proffering its own encrusted fillets of ancillary bed you must break it rusing these spines snap at horizon: lateral curtains before a bald in world take a mark out of root and litter it with heels of trees which scuttle only when plucked from the tips   horizon unbarely renatured at the rips

trunkless prayer
from silted sheds
roofless canopy
in drop-all to
accosted litter

A mesh not to be spared but once again fielding its obstacles, no swerve can deny it horizon now so swept off root, inflects a new groundlessness over everything given: fuller rind granted recognition between anything riven

this outstrap of tree not simply being undone by withdrawn root but active downcrop as the most forwarded wrack of the turn, inflective tremble   bend of tall branch still not in dearth but lavishes direct descent

so chambers brush at the swoop of origin, severance itself was inflected oasis, basal affliction

obscene renotation of
dripped overgrowth, this-day
scenery in blain of
shackle, keyed scales
for showing out
entire branch-warp

Brushed to hard flats but in full stimulus array   strewn tight across non-avertibles of horizon (that won't be overhung) or basal stance according to crushed spine   with petition to the ratio of its litter before which naked horizontals can't scatter otherwise than release of shelter

cross the compass which inflects it broken-towards   more scoured than thrown will be dropped on the rack at lie-out: they prolong any switch to exposure mainly pinched with bind, its unclearable-variable

as brushwood does from fountainous fissure to paid-out scroll, entrussment renders horizon uncrossable, no test if it was all mere surpassing of origin at the derivative break

no other evidence
reckoned towards than
broken residence
room by room
pleatly branch-willing

Brushwood avowed non-totals, avid to fork an elational other rationed to this steadiness in break-off   the lining of horizon whose own eject-tree was too far pre-aligned for any other reject not to be co-fisted, sweepings enlisted

a different flexure step by step but each could be the moment of resorting to brushwood, its micro-flagellation of outtake   having touched the ground, brushwood has no farther leaning point, with ground's barrenness no longer *hunched* against horizon

discardant as ineffaceable, transit via surfaces occurring to loss but not its settlement funnel, simply as much grouting as cordlessly sticks to horizon

woods denature beyond their planting so can refigure wildly among slumped isles of triage, peripheral sift of the offering bit-parts

swags of reclitter-
ing looseness, a shelter
core balances broad
its separals
sinter slowly not
what the brokens enter
but how the bulk
of snap filters

That sharpens faith to widely repeated least cut, shares filling it out on lattice embrace horizonward where nothing greatly rooted would: mediate circumferal outfall of storm now plaiting a lull negotiation of damage   not demolition of woodland but its protraction along the micro-tallnesses of horizontals astretch

partial stripping down once severe underbranch is out of reach of tree, across horizontals that awake horizon: lateral rummage with vertical re-incidence at the debris of core

such pains of marginal elaboration frisk ownness' tree by desealing in dissident shelter the coverts of horizon

spore features
peppering enough
to outroad horizon
from its afore

Whose brushwood fails in district, these scales are shed towards more intimate netting as might be para-intricate once externs of the thrown break by a losable array formationally complete

unsealing of embodiment goes along a tactile peeling of ramification   among its salutatory burdens fluted to channels of inflection   called across by entire excess detail in the littered receptivity

inconstancy of relief finds anchor in own brushwood bodied out of the vertical   as if the vertical were itself mined by brushwood but without retracting its unconditional outspill born of root

a branch by cast
for hanghold,
flatpoise convicts
horizon its niches

Thin enough shed above root, elongated much in thorny undispossessibles   what re-embranches a whole disposal of transitional patter: bright wires stranded in grain until it inflect outlift along its zero-crippled lane

paring down an enmeshed all of it before, lean out of border for discardants to stanch the stunned sharing

without some degree of brittleness on the outfetch (these partials still don't deramify) there can be no switch-strength to conditions of inflection   light fanwork is dry thrift at the swelling to horizon by these intransitions alone

fallen across verticals
in sheer ratchet
of horizon's
lattice by leaps

Low brush more open-mattered than any commons of breaking away: tree stems flop to slash until brushwood revives the injury assigned its innovations to collate soothing   abandoned re-entrant scraggy with unhunted brush

rifts of foliage relodged on sitting lattice, no other blanking of violent shelter   seaming for inflecting at open cleft of separation by which brushwood is sharper naped than cut: how it fans out collisionals as brittle pegs for fear ground is too crimped a scrape

exactly perished not flaking from cast-offs, are a lesser interruption of their breaking start, branch plunder wasn't raiding out of any sense of collapsable array

a margin's drift from
neglect has its own
concision of the
unbeset

As in some long sortie of security, encroaches least where it most atones for contiguity   itself in wave of tidal stakes, disattached but sufficingly anaplastic, in kind with the ingrained contra-swerve of inflection

uncallous brush mere invisible severance taking effect *on* location, laid out for cancelled in the gaps of density, impenetrable but for the inflection

displaying angle astray so requitedly at its bend in given rift became inseparable from what little fell of its no way past origin

root-sprags unbundling at their shaken of big tree, their filaments retread at toss, inflect where no whole tree of it could have genuflected towards

wrong junctives
freshly interleaved
at inflection

bent unhandlings
the twist *in* source

lateral inventory
also removed, scatters
to vertical scars
of its reception

to be past en-
meshing is trav-
ersity led, what
pardons the count-
er-abandonment

3

What is it we turn towards, detached in sifts, that gleans into shape, by lying out (swear it ramifies crassly) on the site of our separation which now aligns locally? What figure against general dispersion kept sentinel over brushwood at its thrown-over? Not merely an horizon of expectation but one of ex-aggregates up to granting, a margin's convection transmitted through fallwood, what there is that slumps openly to a formation arrayed unhung? Severed progressively from root but not resuming it askance, so where there is some delayed draft (of rift) it is not a fore-drift consoling the world for its thready haggle. Not by basis but what is shed *on.* Not ground when what is impounded combs through for it to become a differentially perished ruff. But less browsed for its variables than for its unplural stress before an horizon multiplied by the repose. A reserve weft on behalf of horizon chiefly shuttles beside congealed antlers of this much redundant ramification. Seams of brush indicate drenched pauses, gradual subsistence at a platitude of the broken, safeguards the spur of branchlet becoming gash now clenchless on the broken spar, the very hairpin of inflection. Angles of the vertical cocooned in the diffidence of horizontal intimates but the rake-out does it according to another intricacy, disjunctively layered if horizon is to flux its own contrary pleaching across an already slashed whole (not reducible to limbs of fragment). The decoupling of tree and branch enables brushwood to overhang erased edge of surface. In this sphere separatives are savings too barely scattered to atomise the excess: fierce co-parings are distinctively pressed from comparisons of absence. Towards one bold slice of outspread they erupt out of joint scans: from slivered root or shaved lateral apex. What is gathered is in disprocession but successively breaking onto grounded orbit. Not a dehiscence of tree but how the rate of ramific impetus is serious flake at branch tip. A skysore shrubby strip re-stemmed at the dangerous snap weighting the vertical at its wind-funnel. To wade among shot-offs gives trial to the very turn of branch, how tree-part lists from tree-port, relieving its root across a delta of unsown detritus (abridged-inflected but not reshorn). The tree has to commute to further array from its own uninfected arm, become an horizon's amputee. Not point to point commonality of jointing but in plight of branchage whose distant ground is most of the tread, scarce access to what distills periphery rucked across expectation: slim in drift-form because its plenary anti-scatter had stove it in only just altered in the least. Bric à brac not slighted by any ostensive belt of elimination: trees cower no lower than exuding a dried felt of semi-dispersed sheaves culled from root to hold ajar a filament in being's fissure, that openness past upright post but amid all the after-greens the least of which will issue with infill to a pre-given, ungainly tissue of breaking only towards inflection. And correlates rooted bough with anonymous outclip, tender switch rehearsable as frameless, immensely bordered as original. Minus vertical hood as spilled these nodules, inflect any incursion of origin via spines of the scratch pent-out along to, stark quills of gift. A disjoin cutting horizon *onto* the horizontal, only brushwood performs this verticality shredded before litheness of seam, diagonal bedding inordinate in *not* shedding horizon even when mistaken for a parallel. It is inflection which waves exo-spersal, craggy but unstunted by reason of its gapped take consented. Can the things it is be given to? Yes, not meanly but *to* scarcity, the fidelity-peeling is ballast served rare, the exception which placates a scattered-from by means of a flexed horizon severed-at. No greater observance of inflective fragment than this at increased frisk of its surds. Turning from enigma onto a surfaced poor-base its mystery: this isn't hierarchy but orders of brushwood, not a patter in outcast but frugal meta-abandonment immediately beside (at the curvature of a much localised departure). The active scarcity of blank world ostension riven until rife with overlay. Rootless when ramification post-ascends, now at a late reject/project margin off the scarce baulk of origin not diverted but inflected. Bent branch off branch in branch's giving but inflects it rigidiform, enigma with skimmer will be mystery selected for its sill. Draws to a projective floor original contusion (leaning into horizon) but is partwise cast adrift from the living in sheer stiffness of what can be offered (living too much of it lengthways) towards living out of turn from branch to brush: strictive fantail that is both key disconnection and resolute segment in core array. Brushwoods chastened by their lying across treelessness, whips of caul which horizon vets to coil, at last porous to the wrinkled posse of isolate transects of resumption, trans-protractive. Connective inflection unembarrassed by terminal twitch when wreaks onto-possibly: from indifference of givens towards deferring *to* gift, not doubting already actual within some micro-burden of reception together with a lateral cherish of displacement. Brushwood can then trigger reparable surface crossing earth nests (if brittle enough for a quake at the detected given itself): re-posing continuous ramification at its stopped but unretracted stem-segment, forays at ribboning without putting off the inflect-frondescence. What is counter-lost off tree is how an extremum communicates about outering via a brush-quartering *recognizably* collating at own ringside. Gift might only partially overlap with the given, the cussedness of granting being the more loosely primordial, but so it flies in the face of the inflectional (how givens in their flange of spurn are put *towards* the face of gift). It is scarceness real of any charged relation with givens which enables gifting to break them from their given shelf in order to re-inflect, at the same time perfectly sustaining their primitive fractal invigoration at the figure's stack of taken by accompaniment. This is vertical contiguity strewn to its conducible prone mass. What is given obtains opaquely but as given-to flickers to alight from fragility (the alighting *is* the break) before going ahead with laying out its brief of relations.

Inflection is in offering such parallel configurations from out of non-alienation *at* the break where failed conditions are unreserved thinnest *upon* a ridge of analogy (brush against branch until it installs) thickly preserved. Layering that made it across vertical tips of the same forking. Unaffordable but proffered, thinging into likelihood mapped the distortion accordingly. What the buffeted alive inflects of its life in common with the already given but brushed to anticipate a further lateral encounter along intercessive ruptures of the given. Plurality once givens are ascribed this way wears down the asymmetry, as much as particles of gift go vertical. As they are gift in article to incontingency in relation, the matter of sharp fines of reception. The tree is subject to not belonging to the network it projects but is brushed from flesh to flesh at the woundlessness of inflection itself.

4

forest foreland requires uncaged brushwood to be firsts of
remainder at the assartic splay

bent suddenly at daylight to horizon, a bright fold neo-afraid,
its white slash collects so far towards brittled leave

shedding more attempted than shredding given this
exclamatory mode spreading remote from felled trees their
unquelled spurt

for the construction of a proof space cover the unseverable floor
with repealings of brush

not present at anything less's founding moment, the least of it
had already fallen to a brush with generosity, sheer branch lies
out in reach of its separation from tree

instances, rests, apparent distentions of what divide into well-
crashed things but offer critical feathers of origin no longer
perched on root

horizontal lattice but still offering its vertical torpedo by
poverty of extended hitches, rootless throughout an origin
dissevered towards

brushwood is hollow freight against crabbing the way, its gnarl
slenderer the further, plentiful snag on whisp gives a frozen
bend to the furtherance

slips through to brushwood only coring the hollow itself,
spoiled enigma at its toll in mystery

ex-pendulous devious bracket off rise that by a small inflection
aches the world

inflection out-delineates the spurned twists of forgotten limbs,
exact texture of surface's extreme count of cast tree

the push to woods' event in brush   a singular meta-attics
outside the roof-row (tree ethics) but infusing the grain of
horizon

well sprained and clear of its rank in the upright, its anchorage
peelingly exposed to what ground rasp this marauder hauls to
horizon

no tally for tree loss except adjoining brushwood: outnumbed
by tenured branch oblivious to stump but which brushwood
retouches by hemming so much along the nerve

brushwood traipsing to forehaven (itself post-entrapped,
*re*trammels the single point of its origin shaven)

nothing wholly natural can be sampled under brush, the
branch-burrs off origin now so ample

unadjacent paroxysms are link for limp in what passes for
unsecured between: there are no *uprights* towards horizon

stiff brushwood progressing decisions of tree, cut in on bending
out timber so forwardly at bay

undisturbed brush outside the palisade of attached life, lying
upon such offering for lessness satisfied, free from rootfuls of
the abstention

inflection is a discard's motivated lying out, how surface
complies resignations not signed off from origin

armfuls away from the wrongs of sectioned root, such a fork to
set at niche in the mortise of horizon

weaving by prone tip across a scarcer drift in binding, so
spindle-hardened it cracks out laterally: discard the specimen
and abridge to new commons of trans-selection

brushwood bedraggles the reclined reach of plain, as gift is: no
longer *truncating* the horizontal

the trees' further dwelling of own unimplantable loss *on* load

palm extended (to the planet) which these fingers render, the
stretch already original past cut, unhierarchic parts to be widely
reburdened

to cut spire down to brushwood sweeps out the scuttles of
horizon, a retaining rattle on the turf dries out across such
absolute shelter

what wildly vaults to levels of horizon, a cut-out deeply
flattened ahead   until scattered from tree it trembles to daub
such a tree-recessive bareness on origin instead

broadly disenlarged elapse to field, crosses rift with its inflection
gaff, out to the brushwood there is in gift

in filigree incentive post-severant but little dissemblance,
brushwood isn't matter for any better hounding of tree than
this

wastage subject to host bandage swelling the jut, the gap at
point of inflection or to undress before swaddlings of horizon

straddled givens trans-embodied, lesser parted body of the
greeted eclosion (branch fined to its finish) which to scatter
performs serious home to margin

brushwood more deferring on the loose than it gaps the flecks,
no resistance set clear of the saturate web of consists

nothing weeds out exposure on empty so much as brushwood
falls, this filling disrupt bears out what is *overgrown* on earth

freshly thorned by how resigned from root, gleaning through
brushwood its gaze on mobbed origin, chokes of scrub
impending the loose range of horizon

in scrawny crush to where there is no snarl but origin's

its poverty not to rest in seclusion but be wrestled from enigma
by the inflections which gave it bent until breakable enough for
brushed harbour

as uncoiled clogs enough to liken enfolding, the spring of it
just this jerk to a native plateau brushwood is abandoned to
populate, dry source in hand of

strings of unseizure no barer there in the last brushwood paid
out too near the fall of it to be reamlessly scattered

inflection the precondition for finiteness what counter-confines
by reach the slights of itself, relational debris attended across
horizoned extent: brush the event from its tree

exposure (A Tree) presents

2011

The Tree. It shows what we would call
constraint. It bursts through rocks in calluses
R. F. Langley

You cannot lose your innocence…
…Nor could anyone
Given the right woods.
Jack Spicer

The void that hollows out is immediately filled with the
mute and anonymous rustling of the "there is."
Emmanuel Levinas

Any soft plea is seized at abutments
Mark Dickinson

Note

For some months I had been drawn to watching a spur or outjut of exposed beech-root (projecting like a bracket or congealed vaulting) along a much eroded but little used holloway. Beneath the root-bulge, the undermining had also carved out an embrasure or cavity large enough for a sheep or dog to shelter in. Out of the root-bracket a number of straight young boles were growing (probably the overgrown remains of an ancient hedge), boldly vertical but mainly dependent on the precarious root-platform (and since then these optimistic shafts have been lopped).

As the indurated root had been eroded laterally, a full exposure was primed by the adjacent cavity below: undercut was collapse directly below excess bracket. But the exposure also projected a spur to the vertical which was tree-like enough to present some post-abutment taperings of itself. So that the presentment looked like a lesser-exposed, or whatever proposes the scarce, any silt/quilt within infinite finitude liable to relate towards or on behalf of.

If nothing originates in exposure, this presents itself as a given lack which exceeds nothing to the extent that the nothing is tapered towards lacking its own giftlessness. The vertical is not simply repeatable as part of a horizontal plurality but participates in the judder and uncertainty of any gift to place: as how that place holds itself apart (is exposed) along verticals but which proffer shelter conditions amid the diagonals of canopy. The canopy is a commutation of a root-wedge itself prominent because it has had to adapt to a derived lateral support.

Does such a knotty ontological allegory offend the contingency of site? What is radically exposed is open to the burden of what it projects, and it is this mysterious bundle of unenforced coalescence which lets itself be slightened to all that allays itself presently assisting.

March 2011

I

Quicken exposure and will have it sense a narrows on ledge at loose holder   minimally invasive but with internal fixation pressed hollow   exposure cracks out lips of grain (a re-embrasing), deals root an unspoken shoulder   entrenched in veering through the heel of what held

root acids etch a traverse along the crevice, estrange the exhaustion with cradle   have only a friction of uplift to contort with

roots ticking and stitching across the bedded rip dial from light exposure for a tread of the braid   mitigate abyss in ground crevice, intertwine at a flap of canopy

interior cavity where the basin has fallen away, its grating an event local in tree   large jagged flaw-stone squints until a root is lens by surround, the tree's gathered reflector   close to texture in the flinging stock, a cautious root wings forward of its aboard creviced abyss

grow down the tree
into long right root:
at the end of any
root it uncramps
its vertical haul

Exposure (this legging) ladders, leaving for a face of tree-aisled crevice whose wrap is unsteady at blest   only a stress fracture can pressure this gauge of abyss until it rake sides, whose presentment rinses a hair of it to least clung ridge

cold frame of exposure until the porch of root snarls then cools differentially near ventilation of a present embrace   where density is picketed but hollowness got it more striated, a mat gritted towards its own gap of assertion

post-exposure spillway
how the cull braces itself
for its forced protections

embrasure's incisal edge
splays enlargement pres-
ently rewedge across
ex-aperture's finishing

Tree roots may exert enough prescience to dislodge distribution, as a tree gives a blanket start to the accord of it   cavity cricked by its climbing health, about-burrows towards vertical boundary

tree optimal cover at the deceleration, recompose natural verticals for its own root rate   an unwinding route, how the patch at net steers towards the vertical no longer spooling it

to create a room from a gable of exposed strings, a roof from the globular crests of root

open rack on woodland
prong whose crevices
peak at bluff, re-
pleats for cache in
righted neck of rock

Exposed but no longer bared in tree, circumtenacious bound bracket of an alongside, gone to lateral jib of ground swung with all the poor-store of a vertical insistence sounding out the slights (at height of fissure) above groundlessness, caught to shelf fasting for rift   not for wealth of its hollow but filled levity at a cavity of smaller projection

a stance raking forward what diminishment thins in shared vertical attire   compartmental re-impactment, the texture does so much lean unsquandering at rim   addressive-fissive off root to break into (entube) the rock-slate

how being wedged against a
scoured by support
can spike vertical entail
lateral sheer-face met

at a singular vertex,
thin walls of filled spenders
hang it tawdry
but retaints well

intimate gash intricate
mesh, open chute
is root, focal
blockade at branch

Seatage of root makes suit to sweep the leap, not across gap but hooking itself out of enclave of exposure   ex-trenchancy of a cavity's opening poses a ridge of the hollow to its vertical plane: once swallowed the scallop is shallow take but cushions the event-prop to acknowledge its scarcity secured

junction bracketed to ground but only at its fallen upon exposure: whose rare counter-sprawling leases canopy above a globular bulge because of the root revenue hung far out over the lean as exposure strips to dispensation, this scarce ravage has nothing to slip from its cavity other than canopy

awning root-bundle
on ancillary verticals
callusing a differential
ceiling, asymmetry intent
it perform a roof

rock cavity (but) mouthless
until root retongue it
under canopy

hitched (cavity) until
the canopy latches, skimps
seam up to the door
of the vertical

What will do vertical regrowth with hunched nester on a lateral perch entire above-ground slip of tree   addresses present tissues of treeshaft condensation, spread of protection along each satellite resistance

durable rigid skin sheathing at its outroot channels, funnels of verticals no longer insulated from this lateral hinge   directional gap is a greenstick fraction given angle-join upto a pocket of event

depth of face browed off,
have cavity empty it wide
towards fill of roof

cavity implosive wills
top-girdling, springs
direct yawing
at graft overhang

Exposed-disclosed creases by root at the semi-stake zone of liminal tree, a spiral of cavity for milling at a tree's upright whose from-ground is off-axis but generously bespread at the conversion to canopy: no less a flap *over* the vertical than it gave rootal discharge to random cavities

presence the part by which the root-thing is counter-sunder tall slender, dashed outward at a bracket's husk in greenish shiver   the flattened intent (not root dissent) at a tree's vertical successivity

precedes by forward-spelling lip the next at mount without dropping from root, it freeze-drips upward what juts the headspan from its gap

bedless cavity additional
steerage, how it cramps
(tests) speculative narrows
above root

sands of erosion
give this partial
harvest a hem
at ledge, is weak
union but whose
rake stucco
is basal spur

Exceptionality owes precarious entrapment, its relation made scarce by replete condensations: from root crevice to scarf of canopy

essence of root assists scratch hook find bait on primary shelf, now secures own tiling off horizontal hip   network of root-referrals inducing a world expose asides goes bluntly to its canopy-scarp offer beside

being riven as crack
taken *at*
fixity of the given

until it awns open-
toll from the stutter
upon vertical abutment

Congealing/deconcealing an outspread's contraction along the time-spine, the span (vertical) embosses hollowness until refunded at root-wrist   an all-sides outbed flies under canopy from this abrupt single-recess exposure

spending unmapped the shelter spread from spine because the vertical itself pluralises   sprig relief patina prompt recess over which root makes bulge for vertical accessories   better reposes at strap limb (transitive joist) leaching from cavity as much as it can brink

the sleeve all external but resolutely longitudinal, carving canopy from adjoining cavity's underside   exposing relief to its weathering inflection of branch presage

the flow of open transit
reckons tree interpolate
wild narrow relation,
a mild flocking to station

Trans-reparative error if only at a shingle abrading it binding, offering a vertical from beggared ground   how much spoil can be grazed onto tree and by what seizure spared to canopy?

the sill's forerake's emissile retable's offset wedge radiating a canopy-ear hard of shelter   valvular reserve laterally wounded but sprung on vertical uplet, outvented   a panel of exposure swarted against blanking

where the tree itself pauses onset against further vertical clawing but the respite was always ascending via scarcity to height

crystallize enter stark anticipation, sclero-downsize but severely does participate at the indented take on horizon whose distance had shrunk to cardinal bite   but inseparable canopy is loosely come by

project an open dish
from upward clause
in rock, since cavity
grudge so flared
a tree's own undersling

Irremissible rebone bunged up on spire-stoniness persists in making light of scarcity at horizon   gratingly encysts the granular ruff at its pitch levering a staff

cleft of root in place of veins of gift at waft of exposables
squandered home, but the roaming itself leanest most pendant

significant cones of tree once they re-ascribe to trans-lateralise
the naturalistic scrape of bowers   owing from incentive ledge
to given scarp

threads expose compliance's
proven twist, amplify
a field shaded from
tautness by scarce hold

Robust in claim to presence/decrescence how tree at upstretch
winkles it out of its origin cavity   those further tree-droops
were incontinent but clean of access, then smear on root all the
diffidence there is in a vertical counter-inception

root at the caged splint of exposure   what is hollow indents,
what is dented towards (brace) retorts in canopy

openside chamber hits vertical clamber, turbid chaser of span
from convertible tubes of void   at this apron lip there can
be no further drilling into exposure, the fully snagged scope is
tipped with small hooks towards its vertical coefficient

a knack exposure
loudly intricate de-
pends, rap there
on the loose door
banged because
of tree bedding
above the parted
shallowness

Tree core is quotient elongation out of subsurface (jolted root), a gesture of blot presence long overdue its ramified disenclosure from exposure

what everywhere trees suffer pacing out exposure to a subset (horizoned) presence elision is root film by gift of cavity hardening uprights at an incompleteness scale, then the canopy flex will fully extend over its root nail pins of present residence redressing all that accretes lighter-than-penalty at its plate of ground

less an absence tactic fully exposed with givens out from rock than a logic of root dis-exhumes the debris of abundant arch in tree

safe digression in-
cision creases a tree's shelf:
post-exposure's crimped
transition versus
absent bleed at cut

Tissue unshielded but enlayered, cavitied at exposed bank,
already indurated toward concise origin what a tree
won't sift to explore is root amplification, must locate slippage
remoulded until well crusted at leaf abreast

notch fallen into scratch receptable as in alterity of the
vulnerable: less itself than tree bundle altering the ratio tracking
pouch because shown crevice

exposure not projected but concretely trans-dejected at hollow enclave, willing a present thinning for the arrive-of, the tense of it vertical

exposive to meta-
closive intimately
counter-ajar
recklessly slammed-to
found open

Ordinary woods convey only what we eke out of the ready, a present unheeded flaunted as thrift   underwhelms us we can't stand forth with, no exponent so slight it's not a crevice-filler splicing the displacement, not among branch initially but keen stone recesses cluttered by root

not desert as such but a diminishing before what needs choose host, hamper being *at* the face of its presentment

pelted until sheltered
boldly, it is exposure
which folded the
hindrance

unheaded by its arrivals
but quarried at the
trunking of a favour

Rims to brace spoil-free exposed to being in-store with the anticipation coil   rustle of canopy meshed top outcrop, closet fillet of bough loosely occurs over roots sinking until sheaved

the monodome tent of root vaulting it rife   stumps will do enough verticals at unvexed next-to-present dismay

whose seeding roof tensed, as if abating the abrasive trust   I
think of pausing them through the rift, all shading hanging out
for exposure's fever of root

exposure not waited for
scabs of it bear out locals
a filter of reticulation
outed the side shed-
ing itself within-to

openness repopulating
crown gap, confines it
scale this unmet
aside following all
by-sources it greets

II

Already unsealed from itself but poor enough to steal attached life to a kit of relation, a blunt jerk towards additions of acceptance, copiously sparse, rooted from edge. Exposure flings its extra earth short of the point where there was to be plentiful severance, the commons uncut but now hollowed up to a tooled margin given a keener mean of exception than would ever have been generous to indifference. Distal concavity spanned to plural hold by inlay of root, a resident at rest in shallow parallels forwarding the strings of access presenting guileless vertical upshot. A lateral hollow steered open by such vertical rebuff off exposure. Shored to a snag but corrects high at heading a counter-bar of tree, a well of insurrection whose coping is agile to mild reversions above. Recessive terror flocking to scarcity's project overdraw, counter-hung in exposed face skinned to root but never shrouding cavity's direct chest to canopy. Whose shins ascending were lean prescience or appositional shoot, less with new skin of ground than each tilted nothing-hidden aroused on dire rooting platform. A pitfall encrusted with active stack, the exposure pressing out lateral cements intensely ramified until a slow hearth of vertical risk. Already slighted of so radical a nurture that seam/layer/beam in the crest of its wake will suffer no more faltering entire. Not a many-branched universe until exposure mines it for slits, where root-minority awaits canopy-tendency, shoots of the enlittlement fork broader fill towards their shelterable real. Because crevice laterally bled is the tree's minute exemption, universal dread over razed base but exposed to inflict the same generative span. A root-hedge of imbrications sharing horizon, what arrives traverso-rigid in zest of gripping its filler came with present rearing to shelter. Root travel can't be discovery as such, otherwise any clarity of intimation shies from the sharp bracketing—onto a vertical it was rubbed to be diverted by. Cavity feeds are what upright brevity it can get, on short-stalk beckon from thickening proximate accomplishment but faint before gift. Already anything given (stung) is less than readily there, let alone diminishments along the stay of preparation would anticipate a pro-leaf pall nettling what canopy is to do here. Clinging from hollow rock is itself speculative shelter protected by rustle of stone, shards are pegs where otherwise no gristle of ascendance culminates. Exposure most itself as a secondary horizontal (once the coverlessness is blown) presenting to a tributary of the vertical, the intimacy driven to battening root for stab of canopy. Relative constriction among horizontals projects relations for opening out vertical, where differences are non-possibles of accumulation but any excess is for the growth-smart of a tree wringing out its lateral disparities as hitherto all the clinging it might get (until its singulars are niche-simple enough to survive bundle coronas of shelter). So bluntly exposed, the tree delves more pared to presence of inhabited rift, is a whole roof of re-sanction. There can be no slinking to this edge of seat, just the one pre-position of slide. Scarcity looks to implemental edge, its reduction to taper, what can't be sundered from the thin positionality of gift: where it niches both wound-print and site punctuality. Pressure to be present, towards scarcity's as-nothing being well ramified before bulk enigma uploads of promise. So that a counter-deficiency acclaims the wholly given its drive along strips of the slender real, branch-root-sender-origin manifest by sleight of stand. The opaqueness of what is exposed-to would only take presence to a non-transparency and now as less than any *wealth* that might have been given, shrivelled visibility ripens under chinks of branch. But how any slightness of connection tabled at the exposure pitches its trellis across white lights of the horizon, smitten with porous canopy, whose absorption does in speckled relief what exposure won't exonerate from attendant belief. A ligature that *does* return but its lap of retort equally a lapse of narrative enormity at the tree's brusqued heel of transcendence. Protusion point the splint of it rootal ductiform, exponent bracket at a pin-simple of lift, all space has nothing later in stock other than at once given-to-sill. Bushing up forest bone, what arches across slack displaces vertically, and then in a way not quite loved at its proof until all from root was at a roof-over. Unthronging penultimate scarce embodiment pressed micro-tall to gift. Where a given unwraps beyond relation, gift redeals its care in what is full immersion slightened to commending on behalf of, with exposure admonished (accomplished) in the frank shade re-sparsed by what it shed. Let the detraction expose what it gave out, in a spate of presence to recompress, how slightness encircles a spindle of address. Sacred graft amending its scrap-bestowal in scrapes of perch, starker fitting out of severe inseparation. Nothing bereft of bracket once there is no theft of vertical thicket. Parting the standing grain by offering a surface to roots to outfield the sky, had not the rock already offered this very pitting some impression of air between fronds. Overhung obstacle according to impetus of offer, everything means the micro-paralysis *is* connection, thinnest fastening has a clinging bout *until* horizon. The sub-throw a kind of stasis, a lobe bobbing from its present receptor site which can only reduce to root, a stripling in zest of sapling, inter-crustal gift. Exposure to the rude rampart, dabbing what is promised at an undragged tree never clear of being tied-in towards leaner extremity out. A reception loss unable to *show* exposure to gift sifts other bays of needlessness beside runnels of saddled seed. Nothing can lead exposure if not this graining by distribution, grout of remaining at a cleft of unguarded shoot shuttered by its own ingression, exported to a further flinch of the endowable. A scarcity-partial capped for myriad limit-actuals in immeasurable slight fissures become tissues of gift. So that exposure can never be a defunct assignation, it learns head-on what scarcity waits with at many a singular non-deflection, which *gives* the direction of the vertical. A micro-cavern whose hollows are only shown *to* exposure by root, an excess of rim already raking over the verticals blown to tip. As gift has sequels, is present to this raw by sparing root-pores explored to leaf, healing is well-betrayed enough the better to allay its verticals at canopy transposition, a remission directly overhead for all the ground's equals. Privation allows a spirelet to be consigned from exposure towards retiring in stalk what otherwise appeared preventive: no less spurned (carried) from end to end than is any horizon dropping on penury at the vertical.

III

given frontslider, mendicant mass, the rake in a rib of pulse,
verdure at groundly intervals in a suspended shaft

deferred shallows shelved half-stark, sizing a tree's climax
veiled across the exposure

roots that jump, graft and resheet what is exposed to ramify,
allowing latent clench a re-use of field (suspending) at this
low brink

source-inordinate (exposed) in buttress spent on scarce ledge
at the hip of a tree-ascendancy

brief in verticality but not denied own lateral momentum
an enjambment of spines widely shunted but steeply
havened

leaning out of its thinness of summit a canopy realigns such
fetched unopenables from within the exposure

steep-rooted slightnesses of a tree recognising its interim of
verticality done to gift

twist-table fissure is weaned to open root, its bare profile
dearly insists on a decision of entwinement

assorts its at-presence combed through scarcity of the
unadjoinable, no attainder but in branch respond

ontological outage is observed at a different rite of root—levels out a tree's paring until lattice-scarred throughout its directional load

for ecstatic plight horizontal all surge is towards the emphatic's slight vertical

what is exposed is widen the thing to world, passes through its carrying neck a world's brow present out of narrowness

to expose adequate lag at root tray, the hold gains unentire or asymmetrical its radial loan to vertical shaft

attend vertical and stir it scarce, distance from source is nearest obstination of its presence, gives shelter its bickering dial

now its pendant claw improvises taper after exposure to open bare is to be reduced to a single point of root

rock cleavage bucks the canopy, no enclave gregarious enough not to tether to any other solitary tallness

with scarcity its gifted partitioning in gap, intrinsic spiking up from exposure a root-membrane at a time

injection shade at cavity, rigid at its fabric striplings but which vertically walk away

exposure lamed by blanks feeding shadows of leaf, what a shelter scoured by populated fissure will always run off bars of light cavity directly pronouncing canopy, its aproning of exposure may trap both rinds of making present

a periphery of envelopment encoded laterally but whose brunt of core is to be flexed vertically

presence likes the compression information of fallow exposure in its face

tree nestling the exposure, kettling the composure of blank being, whose sole filter is a present shornness of arrivable content

harshness but no oasis of non-exposure to a given   the etiolated string of origin as much tendril across crack as root in hollow

failing exposure once passed openly out of itself, this fault tree presents admission at the detracted participation

exposure made strange not at its loose ranging across admittance but that this savage profusion is evenly taut at the hollow slights

losing abutted base but resting over it, least crest plucked from rippage until canopied at the woundless raw of it

they are not completely host to us, but in stone fissures dribble the pleats on a refold gratefully swung off gap—whose protractor residue is as canopy to the evaporation

scarcity not in bracket to sacrifice, infusing intricate easing
at the cratered limit, at canopy (to be capped) tending to
catapult a leaf-harness, finals sprung to fork instead of

predecessors by exposure ventilate its leaves out of that
fraction, to the whole rack of presences by friction

because fully exposed does scrabble to a niche of presenting—
may rear a concision in tree (accedes steeply patient) before
an horizon immense at its other than replete

SPARSE REACH STRETCHES THE FIELD

2011

…as if the fields' shapes had been determined by the trees, not the trees by the field.

Richard Mabey

Between the nihilistic promotion of dissonance… and the risk of harmony stretched to the limits… there remains an undecidability.

John Milbank

The trees say, Pull me: but the hand you stretch
Is mine to write, as it is yours to raise.

George Herbert

I

How to stretch the falling short of a tree?   as fetches its
layering of unleashed decompression?   true for the report
of its sheath-fire onto occupied ravage?   to accelerate the
scarcity only as it beckons across

with many novel patterns of collapse, few have the tautness of *convened* (lessened) lack that disabates, uncrates, offers what it has contracted to reach   a stretch of trees margined at their para-universals of destination   gale-picked placid marginals, recessive tendrils, percussive shields

we stand on the threshold of a post-scarcity remit as the city expands faster than its own needlessness of site   at frail stretch at last for patience with poorly endowed patina on any convertible placing   from cone of branch to the field-spasm of horizontal woodland subsumed from outlyer   a debris of fore-brandished choked relay

scarce forest cover but tensile shrinkage   anti-creep by concrete sanction, contrary when and as the mentor of shade overflows sharp vessel   adjacent crater (cluster) of branch cage but well forsworn of root

the latitude of scarcity is to *spring* at pinpointing its fielded world   what reaches the slighter term of any infill, static elision of its retrieval

a deviation settles
rare those raws due

sparse creep prevail
past forest zone

damage obtains scarce
in monotonous levy
of reach, bare-earth
materials at stretch-
percent covering it

This struggle to extend to scarcity its life-staff if across branch stockade from tree-retraction then according its internal (participatory) storm a sparse (wide tersed) application

degradation of forest wave on wave of scraped field the incomplete reproach of scarcity exceeds plenitude along each tuft of reach only an horizon of the enormous propensity encroaches then

pinioned stretch suffers streets of field to run off curdling sheet—there is no demographic application of reduced scarcity save the scars are super-induced at this phase-breaking, the crawl in forest backing

we stand on the threshold of a post-scarcity renunciation—building grows through tubes but not enlivening the wires from their hollow arena of plenty what locally bricked charge reaches it stunted under load?

taut in the silent wood
fainter under trees'
lesser-wooded given
its future batch

a forest is critical
discomfiture, stringent
unaborted sickening

commodity frontiers
premised on select
forest reduct,
package of perimeter

On the crest of scarcity by extendible ratio attaching it   tasking
taut sails of branch, its slow skin sample   now communal
intake of the scant, a march of great plains within contrition of
obsolete blanket   though its tautness assays the untainted, hurls
coils of stretch from its wake   a wintry grove of pinned strings
tightening the event muscle

these are urban tendrils of forest coating however their sparseness
stretches counter to an advance of like global narrows upon any
imitation of the repairs of centre

the single hurt of what the earth leaves remaining in forests, its
stretch across the blunt universals long hyper-afforded, warded
off

now a swathe of pines reaching from poor reserve, stark activity
becoming it, its park of shave-sector reliance

to throw a forest boundary's pending along this brunt   all
disenvelopping-from were it not for the field's presage of a

deferent plunder   urban slivers not plantable short as were whole corridors of stretch given off the unpeopled branches

by grey skirts of allayed
forest that branch skel-
eton attack the
lull into you

forgoing forest gorges this
counter-fetch, but see trees
scant it at blending
the after-shade green

post-extinction and quasi-stationarity   spectral absciss piercing (pins) any stance of threshold along a flat of branches rising into field   the disposition shifts with each constancy of it overdrawn from poverty towards the spare charts of reach   it comes to an earth so unthickly beseeching trees

brachiation arboreal travail   using forelimbs to win from the unspent retention their terrestrial travel   highly suburbanized zones of tree-lagging, a thermal buffer against enshrining grief in the inferential clearing at the sum of its own unlogged maturity

the indurated predicament vastly chipped in time with crust of field to street but tree cover more daring   at its unmassed row in the roads of interrupting from harm, miniscule relief in token of reliance   branches unslacken across a score of terrains more tree than root by no two reaches ever the same in loss of provision, a damage-park by what stretches toward decried lines of the non-abandonment

waves of forest degradation
emanate the major demand
quotas, stretchable not
as radiant leak but
branch laceration
open-knit above field

suppress tree and attune a compression of tree   earlier repulse is latterly disavoidance grappling with flap across the field entirety's self-vacating envelope

stretched at drawn-out fully sparse   reach for minimal reduct member placed for its conspiring dependence   multi-branch counter-shackle, how field the more supply abuts at its branch suckle

trees pencil-phobes by
natural graphic scratch
scarce at a stretch
whose unpacked bundle
scours entire field

II

Wood lightens the thumbs about its thickets and there goes attachable breeze within it, begs a draught of the narrows whose paleness of apex is preliminary baulked limb, what bridges the currents of field

Wooding in no bitterness over sparsity of stretch, encounter of reach to be in the brittle what was not in the leaves but the attribution of their micro-rigidities

Sinews and roots threadbare but stretch their shower of limb for the intertwining, embeddings at unsealed protective paces, a scarce spurt to the pleated surfaces of emergent leaf at foot of field

Stretch them the cost of relation, across a post-abundant array throwing on its cusp further offerable compensation such as the field is starved enough to publish

Tree spindles capped in consultation but at a passage of baggy wind-frappage, from lines of poverty they trail the heeded knocks off wipes of land

The fir's frame is not to be divided from its compression-abject of fit, the leaves it forsakes to stretch a tree

Poorly multiplying its fronts tauter than implication, additional reach in the availing distribution we knew from no appliances but field

Branches not strained but *reached* against their stay, that harrowings accompany *these* framed clumps by not impairing their boxed (travelled) curvature

A corrosion of trees outside their blained element, stretching the portent of scarcity's arena, unvexed by the scant asymmetries, green-tied sieves

World without fail but lacks contractile weather to set out the stalling except it leach to the blunts of it, racking this corridor until the street is active separation of trees formed along its continuous unravelled succession

Greenstick apertures, tipped aptitude until any branchless leaf has freckled it before the hoof of field

Stringent sober stem pitched rigid to what is not lean trim but its granted to remain, foreshortens the grain but voids its own mal-position, deficit of woodland quieting the buffetings of transmitting it taut

Skidded but exact within gaps across the transitional erosion suffering zonal spread, skinnable interface gone green in wrong cage-adjacencies but the same arc a sliver of horizon frets off such bulbous silt entrenched on righted branch

Sliding through field its cocoon impact, sides of compressed body a decoy of pine, each misstep a majority leap between trees, the compass of root brandishes field minus liminal envelopment

a taut deck once
tapped by lean root
reaches joint to capsule

scant protection
huddles abroad, this
is what is press-
ing for transit

Reticence of survival aboard resistance crisscrossing shrunken entireties of the extent, walks a transect line confined to elongated, counter-corridored nurture

A stretched cord of dumped tree theoretically spent on gravity but actively regroups across this uncoveting of field, by common crouch a marginal obsession there is in the grudge elasticating rebestowal

Whose lateral compression was no decomposable, the tree skirt is bloated but toned to the lightness of its after-scape, shares the gradients of littered illumination across field

Brawny knee onto the bar of wood selects trees by no convenient distance, these fibres stun it home, field it with pellets of crust the matter of globules on branch, rewrought fieldward by serpentine (uncrabbed) damage

Such cramped latticing becomes amenably less than its own crumple-zone, readier than transmission for an attenuation pressing for field

What is given does flatness on field off compaction of branch minimals, where there is more absorption than can wrap there is still no relapsing from stretch: fit trees to their field-mark once limbs hatch the reach

Willowy break from stub onto slips sparsely sub-branched, then stiffened alongside any slenderness accompanying the unfuelled full extent, too much to indwell, only a symptom stem of what is offered

Leaping greenly, no split of tree but its scant clannishness, devisiting but undistending the intimacy of field toward its shortspan of cover

Congested by endapplement, which does metastatic disclosure, or contractile webbing will harvest its own interstitial repentance, the torts of a wood in loose gear but with deviant braces

Pressure at shaving diminishes onward mesh, congeals at unarmed torrents of branch, tautly untried is stripped to projective assent, what will substitute for it is not the filigree of its distribution but a trans-waste come to field

In contrast to spent support trees dismember their ample stretch, put it to taunts long past their own bands of slack insulation, the gnarls of its giving leave cascade from the branches until the etiolated corrugation is sparse enough for generosity

Bowing towards another arc of derestriction, matching the limb at full torsion attraction, given the mesh is bereft of side-mast, small population this few at fetching

> a remainder's rare re-
> claimance bequeathed to
> others' ceasing the release
>
> ratchet tautnesses
> by confinement

blowing scales
over the field

Incongruous wrapping about the output grids, reach as it will counter-astound the stumped delay signal, tree-extension girds on a prised number of plates

Harsh models of cramped co-stature prompting field, guarantees reach is expected at its regional ex-trapping, where the exo-tribulation is distance rented to limb

Often a tree-thing pitches and owes, full poverty motivates reactant patted stretch, sparseness contours by less than its own denial, reaching field a relay's long compliance with stop at spine

enraptures fending, twists
in addition the usual
thrust of stretch,
marginal trudge is
sparse servo-chthonic

decrease the spate of
empty parallels but
elongate runnels of
field, ill-fastened
sprigs of induction

compression is self-
intersection, a slice
of brash newly stowed
by forward cells of
clamped (unlimping) trees

Show the green drag (field target) softened on the latch of what it may not closet in reserve, soil doesn't stretch appreciably until reach is no longer shuttered by margins of the overtakens yet to decelerate what is its hardest of field

Scoured particles intend to quieten additives, express flow without confounding pressure relatives, low stretch spanning a far field rubble, one after another this reverse encroachment stretches before the confluence

Absolute serry of abrupt shelter (larch) as with cropped centre, branches (beech) buckling within their own belt, all primaries by extension, unplucked prolongation dispenses to sill of low-pressure ramp in field

Swelling the knot-credit of prevented trees, is what crests at field, a last abrasion of passage has done with its healing

sparse coding for recept-
ive yield, what propenses
margin is not spars
hooding but their skimp
to the heart of enorm-
ous least affordance

beset by noise of a knot
in curvature, its grizzled
bite had no hope of
any *non*-stretch to salience

slight embeddings put
stretch on blind local
field, sashes of focal
trees in kind

prime distribution in agi-
tation of the nest, lightest
on field because collates
      across so few
      samples of it

      every cast bud
      taking its spare
      tree chance

III

acute shrinkage but sparser riddance once before the ductile savour of approaching diminishment to its horizon

stretched from drawn so as not to be a loose chooser, the paucity of assent is fully aligned

novel woody fibres contested on remnant bulk, infill sheer enough for flaking a weakly thick litany off the transitory, its vertical canopy not beset with identical meanness

scarcity not caught in the open but the open caught towards its ramified thatch, swivel the hatching aimed at flare

compression is the intent to retribute from the lesser of its inference all extent of overhang

stoop toward lightened trial union, its snap spent largely but the scarcer brokens selected

string-taut on hesitant pulse, extend the threads of stanched disproportion until the embedding is just that a tree brackets a universal sub-dominant, this is the second sparse introduction but a whole field's revision

a stretch of the unending emerging in singular rarity of the terrain impacting it, abundantly spared to the offer of it

content us reach, scarcely acquire tide, a treeless shore that far withdrawn would have become a field's unattainables

how the abiotic rush upon field will process these slices of scarcity but won't overjerk their residues of life or steer rations from the already offered

this crowded dearth overcoming all scarcities other than the (niche) of it, whose cricks leap by swatches to lessen, bridge its rare connective issue, expensive of nurture along the narrows of further reach

sparse infrastructure to patrol the veering to haven of any less sullen whole extent, tree bones impact as wing struts

scarcity attributes the intimation, taut in given frame smiting gift in reach of lessened states of origin, delays evade field until minutely tangled on the primaries of stretch, *then* comes terrain to unbracket the offer such hard pressing denotes more than a loss of trees but theirs is the stretch which entails an horizon of exact squeeze before gift

preoccupational sparseness pounding on the density of immediate neighbourhood, rarest when a tree limb was not wrenched passively but resorts to the active spindle of its branch curdle

taut capsular shortage of lessons for sources, the slightness of blatant gift

reinstate the something of it across muchness' dearth, too rare for the nothings of it

similar scarce, meta-deficient, a *given* sparseness is no abject compression

or no positive correlation with less, sparse is against *preference* of lack greeting us tauter abroad than is meted out

scarily drives innovation from its slack until become scanter to the life, the deficit of its amendment drawing completely to a friction's graft of branch addressing particulars of the unknowable at source, the compaction presses wholly to extent, but field offers nominal waste for the crease of it

prevention slamming into tree, limbs less wretched than their leaping act, what a diamorphous heap of it was pegged across field

how retracted is the extensional array of tree within the giving tree? all the field sees is a shedding

coagulate lignum poked along slender blank budded entail, stubbed into extension by strakes of its field-making

off comes crisp projection damage with all tapered recordings along the drain of horizon

impossible to stretch a *treeless* rarity, gently taut of the deprivation surpassing it

field can't be offered to unless riven by the luck of its lack, what scarcity seeks and thickens, stretches out a more compacted, missing by no foreshortened ramification torsos taut with indisposables the cramped lean of it dependently towards, a "failed tree" is the penultimate factor of a no longer rare scenario hurried to field

a scarcity latitude offering the pressure its generosity of a taut impression which will only prove porous *upon* field

heavy with unused cradle, their enstreeting shepherds it to such grids aground, these old-growth belts were themselves unsheltered niches but shatter less at a stretch

full shortest-path trees, elongation factor not present in internal memory, has to be fetched from the scanting preview providing the aftertow of its horizon, so scarcity vexes (trans-relapses) its own refusal of exit

taut things abrade the source, boldly its horizon is shrinking to thankful scour, the only spiking it knows in transit no longer perspectiveless for a distribution

taut things not pliable enough to be in secession dis-elide the course of field to ground membrane bought off surface as trees find roosts, the stretch then is common skin due difference of frame

sparse preconditioning wound off prolific supply or branch iteration at a singularity of entrapment, given through harmonics of hampered stretching

unimpoundment under sustained gatherance, filter it on until the dosage is field advancement, true excess scarcely pleads amending such sparse frontage

conviviality of trees in upright foam (rampart crosses field) of the normative horizon-storm, one site ample mantle per stretch

no absolute lack of what meets us (keener than we can be thinned by) until the stretch of it is uncontritional

pent at drawn so as not to lose the fraught accord, but along a stretch of the lack of any trees in the addition

ultra-sparse but no letup in the contra-sufficing, what is a bulk quickening of horizon thriving downward a simplified share of world nature, trees as pests of the enclave of attachment but only as the co-torsion assists a bed to its field

unharbouring twigs upon stretched mesh of the existing, given extent across the entire toll of the given, its tents of shelter plead their collisionless stabs of reach

salient reach only affirmed sparse at field reconnaissance, each stretch shall never be abated

Arch the Apartnesses
/ \
Proffering Trees

2012

The model… is that 'human history' is possessed not, as it happens, only by some human beings, but by a clump of trees

Simon Jarvis

The gesture from the beginning of life
That was worrying its shape into the trees

John Ashbery

Where the borders
are neither meetings nor isolations
but strange mutual insurgencies

John Milbank

1
(Prelude)

Looming the tree under a ruck in the tendon, probes from stock tandem branch angles until beginnings attenuate the step into arch

arch does a taper in uplift towards a vertical event across duality it is horizontals in their traversals that cluster here   overarching gives towards the vertical not to blank off but envelop flickered twigs at a para-tone   what falters fulsomely this way can divert the horizontal

trees not plucked from apartness but shaped onto difference populating arch   how a rising apart arrives across   now they arch it apartward, separatives wood-flustered off the unlapsed (latchless) rencounter

a conspicuous arc of able
apartnesses, a sacred hitch
not unlike fellow trees
deserting from clutch

cloak the long plaitings of these apart-withs   arch-exponent of the virtues of vertical lendings, mingle across the counter-weave

above the closed arch the sheaf of tree is impacted to mark the axis of projection: any branch pull-tab will have its transverse element   parsing the diminishing proven on arch, bifurcation going apartnesses as such project-separates of primal stock, their given curvature over the linear inequalities of arch

arch deck system, both
symmetries fixed to fract bases but
rising to the pressure shells
what branches have to proffer
of their delayed verticality
at cross-diagonals

Apartness of branch its swung area sworn toward arch no other matrix than enough micro-deformities across loose tackle sampled (antiprone) by association geodesic swarms come as parabolas of lift

hairbreadth apart wishing it
between us, each involuntary
socket its which bends, no
clinch to the arch apart
from a curve of adjoining

striding arches abiding the elision by ramifying across incision in one as if tilted branch had been done at the distortion itself

arch buttress to wonder hingeless in apartness beside tapered butts whatever joints is disaccrued by the sweep a tapering quasi-netted pleats in all of it undropped

this apart of it is a frictional meditation (metastation) where the leader faction is crowded curvature singling its overreach into group tension

arch with small puckering
graze off unravaged tree
any crucked angle thickly
negates the leaning distribution

Weak covering of tree property   at its co-diagonal with apartness's outflow, reconcilable less fusion as that more intimate than any curveless compaction

such this unplugged arc of inflection   how non-uniform a divergence from splitting *to* the core that all apartness basins might be re-examined   some cocoon of so many outstretched particles

not quitting from the corners
might mirror the brackets
of a tree lifting (lade-
light) the ensemble

Apartness as baulked attainment, the open offer of a co-occurence on behalf of, no social logic of concurrence   how there can be no bulking up of tree arch   what occurs in not the least attenuated branch shed onto the shoulder it is offering

a prayable of the encounterable giving out at each drip nub of the tagging that otherwise rebibs arch, instead only a tip's end inclining reach about its curve off structural union evoked tribulation (nettled branch) at spike amplitude given clawless arch   any intersection is gleaning the spaces ramped by mutual bypass at tree bifurcate splay

let the arch tool its taper of expanse at a clatter of common leaf bracketing from branch some high contributed apartness between the straying among   until convergence is a precise trans-election (thin section) of the unmet, entirely twinned out on behalf of

2
(Passage)

An arch is two weaknesses which together take a length of unforced shelterable passage

arch shadow we think of as tree tenure going apart from anything clung   hanging across with no couriers of attachment   even here the trees will have pulled the flaring closer

seeking through tree lattice its arching vessel   from stubborn mast to peripheral unlinking   exchange a lank beady branch across trans-dappled owing   there is no such heading as a *buried* arch

paths through veiled
holes in trees, at last
securely between
what is under trajectory

Unbeknown arch attributably legible   the standard property of apartness dilations   a ground's path bracketed and lightly draped

after surpassing platform there is much nearly banded area never made over but already infested with crossing boughs   as with any centrepiece the tree becomes more troublesome   vault-belated, more suspended at the micro-abrasions greenly corroded from any ratchet of relation

stepping unstrapped
though arcing the career
only its gap of onset
puts mesh above brush

overarching sprung
from the human error of passage
planes the perches jogging the span
until wandering verticals
are capped unspoilt

Directly fronting free junctures into their archway   pre-apartness alternating in beech wood knew no other departure for principal passage at the vertical traverse   gradual tongues of an apartwardness after averted concision

the sensory reality of our world is a parting of common stock vaulting the shared, arcading awkwardly   axiomatic braids over mutually pendant last niche

allow humps of beech to be meadow-thick towards their vertical tilt   curvature of poles inhabiting veered particles of every apartness lacking bareness across   foraging /framing what can never be screened less than passage

scattered linear orderings
are paths are tree auto-
scenic are a twiglet
sifting the length
no slim covering but this well-
kneed arching replay

To be in and under the hollow of trees should be less empty than the occasion's obstruction they prove wise curvatures of—broadcasts the offer thinning towards a flex of resource more flimsy than excess taper   what sieves a passage to be under a midst of

a harness-map but at the further hips of tree relations   constant saddling to arch of their non-constraints of kin finishing at continuous vault   florid curtains of defeat of stance just where the juncture gets it away   underscarf roof-scent across outpaced pollen of the tree-tendrils, its basal shower

passage is temporal exception bending between diagonal rests given to tips of the times out at inclusion's way   the sprung-apart scintillates before a choric window of light exemption

exilic road projects
like particles its underease
or between-arch to sense a
beginner greenish hue of
elementary non-exile

sturdy a-partnering
elate if following
holds of it these for all

But three or four such slips make for a gantry evincing it   the undervaulting has numerously evaded its single losses at horizontal   any crucked angle quickly elongates its leaning distribution in thickening divergences how the stretch is for arch sake, a touch pleading shelter at a kink in the vertical   no network is such and such, filigree quakes at the leap of not quitting its own minutiae but opening to standards in spray exactly onside its unshed (ushered) failure

archway treading with own staves now they have fallen away—trace of what it needs must transect with interrupted timber along wands between spaces of coupled air at its vicinity of want of vault

how the arcades leak path around a concrete thread they are not in sufficient standing over, gives to bias zone such fingered plates of penetrated foundation

no post-emptive arcade
all beam at vault is pre-
tenoned along melt of branch

clustered reach but in
sledged grain of
massed foreporch
so all passages accost

it is as every path
meanders through
partable specifics
of incorporation

failure patterns grieve
(gave path) under
huge bristle of arch

Down the path by lift of (arched) central blocking   no permeation other than being undergone at a stand of beech—the weak silt allays onward through a mild frontier filtered to overhang

knots in the path untwisted lightly under these leaf gantries—but where neither path-breach nor tree-stretch is any untying of the entry

a lane cordoning its penetration slant through the very lure of access   any momentum is trick of arch intriguing the surface to over-veer itself, a flicker of the cordage trampled to align   or counter-sampled in arch

species of scan will beam the path off height, the genus is lesser branch segment by extension   how alternative load is set on its road through arcading thrift

tortuosity is to path
as rate of retwist
throngs arch in reach of

a force-free coronal
arcades the field
due its sheer overgrowth
once startled in passage

run latently
steps will walk the graft of path
these lane changes only occur
at a crouching arcade's
riddle of level
via (bridging) bud

Path analysis along kernel traits   a fickle inversion of root into tall dissipation up a well of veilings over branch   but expelling themselves over core cross-venation in condensed vault

whose hollow assaults are not accumulation in brush but minor rickets of sediment dealing out such dissimilar pegs of stalled spill

installed interstitial flow of path through summer intents   no located filtration foremost other than flowering the throughput apartwards   any slippage from arcade is still spired to a lateral summit of mending the content

sieves extensor trunkal to a voluntary unstacking at apex of arch—all the lateral provisos of branch treading its ascent

weak breach
but a long spine
tenders the co-involution

arches to arcadian
can soar over
mere sliver of site

there is no figure of
passage so staked
with marching it back
from branches of untied
neck, collar erect

Tree-augmented native simplifiers where the seam throw is not yet loosened towards swerve of leaf at each web of branch duplicity   unstoppable singularity is being swung-loaded over two for the commons of catching apart

where it is not same duct of its stretch but plump ration as co-ordinate breadth at the same vanishing-tilt   tapered beyond secure transmission but any passage already meted out is sheltered into attempting a lip of its motion   let this be its least liquid bridge, traversing drops of snap solely across authentic surf of arc   responds by not affording tacit alternatives of branch evading (parading) even these brackets of it

swept ribs allow reversed cantilever   tapers according to intransitives of tip-end what gets packaged to send across arch

knotless in rig
each limb co-flips
towards tie it
not as knit

appositively with way
branchlets prevent
all solo valleying
along main arch

3
(Pollard)

Slit under aptness a turn through portal   inverse arches of the
pollard bowl whose V coppices out of cup or a trenchant stump
invariant to radiant   cut multiple uni-verses at the bolling's
occupied blain

a remnant of set-before hollowing but clothing the slash through
a neat scarcity at its inexhaustible   in no lassitude of renewable
arbouring but according a complicity of single-notched
intermoulding

every arch pre-dominantly pluralizes the shadow integration
between pillars   dia-verting sacrosanct codification of chosen
hump to vertical community at the rehealed over-reach

tumbling of what trees
have most in stock
across a craning of their
cut towards
rebodiable

Inverse arch of the pollard tusk's branch cup   spidering across
the cure towards least fallible curve of outlet   or the hollow
fork which tries for cup but whose only whole tallness is re-
enclosure at this maimed selection fist

though jaunty access will spring to a finesse of passing beneath
the disappearances of strap into arch   from the severable to the

tip-evidence of severalling these unpurged margins   however
cleanly turnable in cup that scours round these departures

leaning companions foaming a contrast of rest   all it doesn't
forearm at its elbow of retention, though let presage be diverted
here until forming a net of it as sheer linear threading of loft

coppice howl that cups
its alarm, surpassed bulge
still shafted on an
ample pump of holding

Two perfect vaultings wronging the way up of a lime pollard—
can rotate laterally as each limb gets trans-paired from arch-frame
to arch-frame or leaps diagonally across the regular indentations
of its random symmetry   structurally precise cause-wires
crossing as they will

perhaps the arch layer begins at the defeat slippage of an underling
branch leaning out prematurely   can't yet be proffered of lapse
reaching a caplike unbisected

near-vertical arch-play is not the cure of its pollard wound but
a trans-thinning with scarcely diverted twins of the exception—
cresting is coupled on poor lean by the vertical subsidy itself

the cut becomes its apartness share-out minus frozen precisions
of shedding, a meta-gathering among the poking beaks of cup

the bolling doesn't pine
for its candelabra but pruned
to elaborate cull
re-quickens the wick of it

explore within-tree
lance (launches) compression
recapped at a hub
of coppice effort

Post-fracture zones to expand at the pulse of pollard carping for countenance whose slenderness is primed out of hulk at the resorting knop of inverted apex knack of an intransient index let the retrieval be on call, along whichever wound it solidifies the intersect

4
(Rootal Curve)

Every moment aparture-ridden re-embeds the core across boding
the stretch   to create (sub-filter being no superior weave) the
integral commonality of that minute co-avoidance which blends
a population of gratuitous hinge at horizon, not groping for
caress of harness but caring for tinge intimacies at the tail-off of
reach   this cradling is the awareness of arch itself

a mortise of root lifts through trunk to swing at a fan-chapped
escapement   variation of root cramp finds the dissemination
lightly protected   attentive at an underarc hollow   now the
pilots of its segments navigate tenon ahead of joint

knot projection to-
wards extended diagram
of entire bone spur of trunk

Trees are dangerous enough without these patiences immediately
fore-arcing minus horizontal fusion   but bailing out (across)
according to a refusal not accepted by mere non-completion—
flight of correct adjacency gliding away from the horizon's loan
but insetting the leaning over towards it

all under bar
until relieved of any
thickening, a quick-
ness scarcity of means

nothing's separation counter-
manifested in ramification

filters forest into healing
colonial arch, like real
trees pardons the
stem-feathers of it

Environs a preference lens for sneaking across trees in a convex fineal of near symmetrical silence but ajar at the touch   mutual to the open shudder of meeting: more teeming in branch arches the backwash of union as an express surface of non-interference in the outreach

similar sources vindicated under the freedom of arching a united without joint   against newer pre-apartnesses, this is agreed cluster of edge stalking edge   enfruitment by taper rather than droppable swell to plug

and from the hollow trunk of old trees this refers to the trusted allowances of its emergent poise of roots   the noise of cleaving to lateral confection long stood-upon once blurted above its poll: above the stress of bearing perpendicular hulk to ground   no better non-ground engaging portion of the curve of root than its plight at diagonal reception

let it be a strong apart-
ness elation if billowing
holds for all, mended onto
open truss of arch

retains leaning across
spire through participles
of its lengthening origin
but there is
no *lunge* in trees

leaves fallen from tree
at a bagged-free of
ditching all such
shrubby appurtenances
bare arch was
bladeless all along

Scoured universally by huddle of relation at its non-removal before wave exhaustion: where it hobbles sending-on the slenderness of target, intentional mimic vane assailing the micro-contacts of arch until the vault knows a fully veiled

what is incommunicable in these lets them have us pray arch in them: authenticity astounds the allegory   perches our articulation of jointlessly proffered frame arrived at minimal tassel of rearing over a hyper-requited between

how each shallow pen of root broadens along unstubbable arch detected at horizontal step load   plume scale (leaf market) dipping through ascendance towards a jetty of reimmersion

ration me across
is shelter netting pro-
traction from the
least inroad of trees
given off countenance
that root can't con-
geal into awning

Not planted into arch because a tree is haunted by the indirection of roots   to be a profile of corrections thronging a curve that any overlay of horizon will commonly secrete (loosened) among concluding threads

curvature is each spandrel twinning its precision   post-tensioned as soon as the columns have shrugged upward the gust of root to a bare sheen of unimplanted roof

there the overdue episodes arch from any central stack where a root bundle beams across its own clotted unwrap in sleeker columnar transmission   vertical gift has it sifting into, diagonal accord for each inured intersection

folds of arch
on passive earth pressure
counter-attained within
the bush of roots

branchial axis pulls
decompression finer
if envelopment is
how the arch outridges

by infinitely generated group, this scaffolding is not the spare product of surface swoop over buried root but the tract of it sheer to modest at any lateral-rearing tree summoned to its arch—lengthening filter at the branchial smelt whose weak fringe is sediment to crossings but foraging for pressing out inventions of the impingement double leader drop crotch   as a pontoon will only ripple from origin and not take root-weight from any gravity of ascension—the flotation paddles are not arching any resistance to their dearth of bravura at the transiting motility   where the apex of transition is neither diffusion nor inclusion   what the archway can't reappoint once straddled at a compound obstruction, not to be disappointed at the peril of abandoning singular construction

given such arcade expectancy, a root is unsheathing its host coil onto last elongations detecting a bed of overhang   until branches spoil the twist (already knotless) by grappling a co-encumbrance adjacently infested with arch   where apex is latterly as much counter-arrived as all that proxy scatter

trees were for satisfying a single rudder of root between what bristles there are for scratching out a surface snaking across the disturbance   until arching is forded by shallows abreast of every impact current, direct tide of shelter off the drive-eddy of king stem

contingent the tethering around blunt twig stutter once reliant on arch   self-fencing (rather than shutter) is what launches tentacles of the offering   secure assembly only at the hatch (striation) of its open stabling

that root comes out of its own soil's vantage sieve is in fact an updrain   so that arch can stay for such attenuations, coalescing at its branch-filter off the cascading subtraction   on behalf of its lateral tribulation, an ipse combed from differences of opposing passage   allayed at its re-asking for givable flexure at such an unofferable quaking of stable tenure

blatant armature of compass
little more than tree-petalic
as biased off fragrant
serries of elect branch decks

so mere the respects thinned
from stretch, a cluster reck-
oning apex where luck
of semi-binding (no notches)
buds a texture across

Prayable slips from stem sign a proffered fabric of beseech in research of   but thatch at arch is to goad an overhemming along eaves   no brimming is allowed to be so hook-free unless gamely uncementable by a lolling geometry on behalf of

press it out from inland
stages in salvos
though ligament free
strafe with green score
these hinter-associables

is for resting in risk
any uncontested allergy
of arch compelling itself

in ease of apartnesses
stood to betweens

HOLLOW
ALLOW
WOODS

2013

Note

The shallow quarry which forms an under-bowl to woodland which caught my interest (in an outline of attenuations and vertical counterstrikes) is the flat hollow(s) of Mear's Plantation. This lies adjacent to the early 19c Splatt's barn, beside which were originally two late 18c "eye catcher" estate cottages, all of which are now converted. This is half a mile or so south of Hillesley in Gloucestershire. The standard succession for abandoned sites is tall herbs and bramble shrubbing up into secondary woodland, mostly silver birch or sycamore. Ash, though, is often the first to colonise former quarry workings in particular, given its light, airborne seeds, though the shallow roots of beech do well on the quarry lips of thin limestone soils, as here. In this quarry the current predominant flora is ash, sweet chestnut, and much (though not dense) beech with an understorey of old man's beard, hart's tongue, woodruff and shadow-stinted bramble.

One day when a field of pure pastoral innocence
Caves in mid-most upon a pit

John Milbank

It was a matter of piercing the silence at the bottom of this crater

Walter Benjamin

Over the earth
is the Dome
of the sky…
            terminated
by the exercise
of holes

Charles Olson

1: (quarry / extraction / pit)

The scrape that leaves on itself a scope it may not disembowel   growing within a matrix of bare ground   the scarce put to a high proportion a focal deficit out of supply of its own winced randoms   suites of disturbance-tables for incoming plants

extraction wasn't wide enough
for infinity but stepped bluntly
local down a flank
of absence

a small tide of trapped
arrival slightened
to renewal

collapsing the curve of
intimate vacuity onto trees
transmits a different
ratio of insistency

swelling the restriction
a basin glistening
what loss it might have
not seizure but swarms
the beeches' slow sap

Deep land-sagging (via energy transfer) ferries trees along shaved coats of limits   the vacuum implodes just at this reverse motility   any change in the pit must patch it to invasive counter-fissures   emptied from lateral belt but sending off runners green enough to re-indurate vertical stops along recovery

Swell with pores the scar of the violation until it admit leaf-fallow, just where the operative wound is not repentable   forest pilfer churned into nesting possession of an away-gain, how trees come to a co-sapped counter-arena and curtain loss within its own curtailments

exportable quarry
re-infringed by trees
secondary exploitation
reburdens the ab-
cess contours

a correlate emptiness with
plentiful detection
assailment of seed
finding its doorless way
to uncharted protection

marking a dipped void
retractable towards foliar
bids off its fibrous (mottled)
elation ration by ration
bold shelter model-
ing bare removal

After the extraction any travail is taken too, remains only a contrary prevailing empty of amplitude, the channel of migration becomes unbridgeable   woodland will have paged its turn across sheets of bruise of which this unreferenced hug is the only memory of a corrected to similar linears   roots compare eroded banks but no paradisal slide outward   hasn't ceased resuming a moundal earth in lumps to misspent infilling

What trees are not is a confluent inflammation around wound or self-similar bruise given to forearm intensification   trees simply (unamply) defer not to missing surfaces of contour but to that presageless canopy-additive grafted on the taken-away   where broken quarry gives lip to a workable sliver of leaf   festering enough in wraps of leaf to be proportional loose bandage

what is secret in the raw
pit grated prior gets
restricken in pained
foliage, despairs
made adequate to tree

sample pairing of leaf
before light, a set of
filters at a zone
drawn by the open narrows

disused stock of quarry
running into stick,
unglues its voidal collage
of flat furnishings
on collapsed shadow

Tree kindly a-horizontal collation of mutables but kept intricately sky-cored by a gouge done to degraded boundary of origin, by a sunken (uncontainable) platform   trees here co-verminous with shorn givens where the cleft is due extraction over again but forking itself in secondaries   onto absconded verticals, a prayer-sapped revision   a bleak concave glazes to frontier woodland seeking it out by flashing some other attributable contrition

Any primary reduction calls for its trail of tree aggregate, no culling without this visibly dragged abyss   secondary woodland revising conduits against cancellation   offering the disgrounds of grant its own migration from the outsize but into upright cleft   a bowl of non-extrication chiselled to enough vicinity by this patiently unmatching extraction

sung out as so un-
dangled from un-
fixed (but damage trans-
fixes) origin

detoxify the inspun
rigour of deep box
each trunk is one
shard toward distant-
iating, not splicing,
the entailment

siphon root membranes
away from particles
of pit, feed them the
branch numbers
of inflatable cells

No verge of this subtractive crater other than trees realigning a tract of void by bracketing the vacuum of deserting   suckers of similar forage as grossed-out loss   a fall into reholdables of the tipping across   salient currency through the rustling gamut   of trees of leaves not toiling for ground but a spasm of stream-ends racing into the limbs of occupation as they work over the depletion massing

Absorbs enough of the entombed light to be a canvas over the crevasse, how trees release the *offered* nothings of it if they daub their stretch across   this bringing a no in the thing out of its extraction hitherto an entire pool pulled to loss is a webbing wiry enough to take the strain of formal sacking against any bare ascription of light   where no further eroding, no future corralling of the test   if any intract gap of isolates, then this corrective density

thick as a throat of
flat quarry gets
to spitting up trees

a rabble of shoots
not to be stripped
for the scorings out
of an unhampered
fully holed earth

whatever pit it leaves
is bare-branched onto re-
appearance at a no long-
er staring lost content

To force the thing that forced this shape to enring the pit in no other annulment than spending foliage stolen onto it   whose disburdening finds common craters, the wildings of hope below a ceiling of beseech nil increase but proffers the shrivelled enormity through it

At which above and around crest themselves   from the droop span below surface   fresh exaction according to a single-display exit, fruitage of the crouching seed unit   where nothing has been spilt but how unsealingly   stone once unroofed is shaken from its finished flowering at surface   this is what comes of being taken under covert

a monostorm of absence
caught at a culled void
multiple templates of minute
accent finding next
lignins of trust

trans-seething does these
(servable) underlings
where basal dust gets
lifted out of
any neutral sift

emptiness goes the falter-
ing surround by depth
of width and occludes
unless filtered to its
obstacle within trees

A world stem not always concurrent in a scouted crater   the point of these absents declining to a pre-wooded but already procures touch-down   so why must each insinuating relief overstay its leaf?   what has left us with little in hole has comprised us naked to world as the lesser there is to lattice across the risk of it knitting

But there is bareness here, neatly yarded enough to be additionally discarded along an inference of standing up to the meanest kit of growth   stone after removal creates this newest coast denuded of risk but any raisings will surprise the danger   why it pleads to be able to need trees assail any blast above parapet   stone pegged from its basal splinter, runs it post-shatter past feet of trees no longer confining it to the blank refuge they dropped into

deep-snubbed in box
potential truss of issue
but whose snagging
was always tree-alike

self-undoing quarry
put to fresh crux of
clotting it abroad
a crumple-spate
of front lanes
to the vertically local

scarcer woody where
screened by low tide
attaching distorted harbour
whose insurgence lifts a rug
over a bag of pressure
how is this emergence of
dwelling along spine?

Here the bramble of initial assault traps out a deck for the quarry on which to expunge any *un*shadowing renaturalisation   no cascade of absences not already sapped at scrape, its flatness resurrects exhaust foliage   here, without pasting over, simply root through the brambles, a rich spend into silt   the quarry may not sail its devastation except as resquandered plant abyss chaste enough for ramific swampings

That there can be interior knots for an already outproven site, tight branching from vacancies welcoming the huddle   actively hatching the rifled shell, trees the hinges towards a fresh baulking   on behalf of no unseasonable bulking up   tree/stone as another between inhabits this liability with disparate relief   won't sin against void but flex its no longer sinuous pocket of abyss

stencil-flecks of repetitive leaf
but not imitating the pit's
sheer fallen open

in a soil of no payment
a mesh providing for
circuit trees
stoops among
but staddles foremost

fit emptiness of ground can't
scan a stable wound
until trees wake the
painfully distinct
spars of attachment

Wanting torsion to bundle to the surface what's lacked onward in pale remission   any residue is eventually a permission of trees   even so blunt a project as branch-end will not undo these respites   the quarry may not sail except as blown into mast, so shrouds now all its bluntings by the dome of it risking upgrade between the shoulders of the vacant inscribed toward another tendon in belonging   approach in seed

Trees into limbs alerting what foliage spaces abide refractive cancellations but the loss only knowable in earlier measures of subtraction   bare structure awaiting in the lessened beds its over-pinnings   restipulates earth through its stranger woods

chastened yelps of the en-
tanglement cornering a
void already pitched
to another tang-
ential fashioning

tentative claws of trees
overstay their timid
pioneer straying

maimed to a target of loss
but affixed to a vesselling
in siftable hard tissue

instructive voids at a
rote of desert seedling
then climax dishevelment
revisits ramifications
straddling a blip of light

That the empty of stone is to be tossed toward a tree supplement, no other interval than this   to be a local dent out of step with its ground rock   defers to a null henceforward nil crushing   steering from a rod to fix things into sill   the escapade is slipknots in trees filling out the prior drabness in dip   no concave this raw once extractable, how trees flex their superadded seams toward the off-glow of convexity

A stouter nudge is disenclosing stony vent   for rough para-locations of the sent away   is it a sunken site of the world which pits against any product-transfer of vertical slightness?   or was it too heavily dropped for that retrenching invocation?   the void proffers an out-of-stance but has long since been cistern-heavy with the shade-acute density of another need

translatable squat nurture
of thanked holes
to risk boles thinking erect
amid unprotection's
kneeling surrogate

plunged arena of ordinate
extraction, flanks hubbed
not ridged, flatness
of sink calibrated upon
other flotations of
profit removal

insecurely sprung-from
offers retention at a
variable compass of attachment

Storm-lipped, sonically lean planking gainful across cushioned stores of void   no replacement of lost stones according to such a solo-absent remand   self-pinning micro-forest but as deeply into the matting of recurrence   the good of browsing a wound curtailed onto trees: ancient violence intimately definitional, painfully implemental   tubes of wind-screw oaks in the dependency grain adzed out of quarry   the most supplied wreath is a cloud of seed-heads

Lightly inured at peak foliage to being wrapped in a foxhole   because there is no more burrowing into remnant stone than here   no entrance to the extraction source itself   which could arise only from a revision of the offer, or have coped with being basketed out of itself   no more stunt growths, having already elongated the pit platform

trees don't nest in the
quarry but are the spares
for a more maculate delay

its very plunge already taken
up, this is not openness ajar
but a void in a shell not
of its own making

the loophole given sticks
a forage flecked in scales
of counter-serration that
skies will crank whichever
is crisper than emergence

A negative enclosure made negotiable by transit quantities of loss   but scratched at zero   such micro-abridgements short-root towards the belated traction-trails of trees   the only aftermath is what incoming trees do tail off from the subtraction   not covering over so much as conferring a renewed leanness of ground   what is exact to sky but its non-piercing   only apparently hewn in what puts to stalk as topping the outside of this locus

Knitted over with unpicked lids, whose leaves have their own planes of frequency among absences in sift but from which nothing drops onto a main desertion's own narrow crowd   a fitter way to sprout from a like this, unwarranted removal is to brush it up some minor thing   which will not be enough but offering from new fibres the scales of the desertion

least infra-swooping
what the trees nose
out of hole is
more than its neck

cheap nature has delved
into scarce nature, how
the hole is shallow flawed
before being flared

sectoral hunger for a stem-
specific counter-pause
in the very setting of
exhausted contribution

Welted yields of self-selecting trees of the appliance roaming over an unemployed absence   as the prickle of take-up will comply so far as tree-durables   now end-stopped on a tonality of participant closure from accumulations of dispossession or a source at its vacant rank among brute depictions of trees   a world turf always antagonistic to any reflex of discrete harm   once so shipped off at strip the delving goes relay-specific   precision-repercussive off the dead cycle now no longer cheap hush   becoming a crown of trees' upperleast

2: (pit / hollow/ trees)

Can this gouging (how stone goes apart) be hollow enough, not shut down on its assault signals of alien servicing, unsown for unthrown? can it recede enough to sense the bowl of itself, draw back on its damage? which a restoration (metacontortion) by no companionable content might infill?   not to crouch behind off-laded space but engage in the stiff verticality of its blank obsession   nearest redressed texture mirrored toward what the skies wouldn't shed were it any flat sink

expectant deep void but
harrowed out shallower
to be an offer to
hollowant free-standing

bared to area acutely
susceptible successional
rages of bristling endowment
raw base pitted out
for a play of hollows

a hollow infilled by tree
refraction achieves its narrow-
ing stage,concave waves
jogging a crescent to apex
amid pre-tabular
amples of sky

Trees prick a way for attentive cross-ply but are not the fallen into area— serious with hollow is what out-jets its landzero with negative rump but nothing *overtly* moundal could ever be steeped from uptake of trees this way   woodland compares itself to ceilings of admission, prepares its hollow for a well-set gone missing

Where secondary woodland inducts a diversionary infill   scabs after void via scoops of stem plugging into the depression   enscripted with a fore-bowled it scribbles an assignment vertical in peripheries of resectioning smooth rigs of assuagement   the hollow itself more like a bag-drop onto counter-assailment

no mouth for trees
a hollow is deserted
transience crossing (too
thickly creasing)
absence

foreground frond strumming
the wires until they distend
unable to occupy except
along vertical brittle-
ness of extreme shelter
in the midst its con-
denser drumming

Until a hollow is further stuck (studded)   the earth as friable tree-layer slaps departure aright in short deepages   then swaps every escape for a root of the crushed deposit no longer stubby if much more scarcely stocked   now at last it can be baulked as hollow among woods—branches try out the giving pieces able to rub in even the micro-violated dazzle of descent   almost no remainder as blunt finder but sharply open to transverse colonization   taper towards the inference a relationally lacking thing and attract vernacular burnishings to its reserve

A cocoon does indurate but also webs growth flush to it where the intermediaries of stem and diagonal correction tingle all this disbulking of earth   otherwise immersed in an empty caption (roofless cavern) given through an unwinking eye-socket of vertical barrenness   towards which trees put out their flickers of lash, scarce in the blow

once hollowed there can be no
further bulk quelling, do it
in coverings, scantlings,
encell the thrown-over

no woody walls within but
given porous lining
the drain is to drip it
vertically, any reparative
entwining is equal-
ly cast away

bowed and focal void until
hollow lend craters of dis-
parity to the disposition
of trees, how they abate
the storm of distribution

Rethrown in fringe, a gouge of projection shelter-prone   even before the lunge into foregathered insurrection   the crown skyline records no unevens of loss   releafs the absenting production of essential grout—an uncleft emptiness sharpens the gulp grading scenery-waste itself as it descends *with* a para-surfaced (still chamberless) earth   a depthlessness relaxing from skin will have plunged below its own currents but in the service of pillowing a hollow

Cover won't lurk in a passive bowl but stalks active daylight-twilight across its biased weave   the transmission trans-pittance defrays a lacking extent once frittered with vertical spur-arm expense   by way of repaying the location's gainstay   only the subtraction (impervious ex-product) could be so openly re-askable   bloating trench towards awning itself among trees

through-formed querks of oak
stack off this one confession
wronged at depth though
several rungs up amid a
nestling claw became canopy

austere notching of ab-
sence can't be further
botched by pegs of tree
tuning to hollow before hole

the hollow at a recurve
has no future retention
than the brush of its outcome

until confinement pushes
a focal continent
at shoots to horizon

Stowage columns, sent furrowed toward bark, amidst cuts of rocks that have no other interval haven than this hollowing at every stope of their missive wound   no quarry feature adaptive more than its debited hollow adoptive   only to be partly orphaned once reoffered along frayings self-batching with scarce trees   towards tall horizon as the tousle of its filigree

Nothing squats in the midst of guileless void unless hollows a layer of intricate tackle out of the way of itself   cunning of branch at a longitude of members   if this is to allow itself at last there will be fewer withheld packets countering as sheer twist the vertical risk of thickets

crazed-open quarryscape
a treeful it takes from gap
to hollow, pitched foliage
relops the prelims in
herbage, a tip's oasis
once ex-quarried

these nothings of evacuation
don't break back into hollow
until trees draw it down
attachable blanks seepage by which

whatever is adhesion to safe
bay where the goal is re-
apply gaps as corridors of
outbreathing—can this be
rectified by fallow trees
already recruited through
too open a gap?

Hollow not fillable unless claimful inlet accosted a reflectance-band: what leafmark on horizon does at the next stint   too damaged to be renunciatory but harried along these other successive tapers above surface   a profile rash across the horizon's own milder caverning   a lightly repercussed long arbour of the insufficiency makes it hollow or tweaks our attention from the leafless   onto a deferent openness given with brute twig

Not to outgrow a gap but sieve it otherwise   no more satiety of empty walls but towards an unsettling safety of slender means   the quiver of unfitting it creates a herein on terms with the far-over non-scattered: secure locality in its homing to damage?   trees bend to the pace of a hollow out of gash   face-offs a trait of the crush against mesh   carved slightly but more directionally clad towards other breezes, bitten sonically enough free to do so

deeper outscar of the shallows
of hollow now grooved by
a tense bush across
no longer diving leaves

gravitational deadlock
but stripped to homing
the grounds skimmed
off its pulling to base

blatantly exposed floor
never yet cramped enough for
bed, trees to remake it
from its airless blast

as a rack of root
finding stone, can be a
reshelled gall at-
tached to hollow

Hollow not as flushed-out simples of void but at its tributary emptiness on location   a new laceration of need begins early towards full slice along any plausible stem, enough to arise as a contiguity   nostalgia for green towel has its own (   ) corrective when stumped up with gnarled wraps of a low-pressure erective

A hole so upgraded is a hollow inciting reflective gristle groping toward survivable induration as outrise rapacious via secondary shadings, given project to an already violated spaciousness of the foretaken in place of provisions of cancelled stone but not deaf to leaf once sonically raised in tree

bind themselves to bowl
while sited on own tackle
tapping a hollow out of
consent, not wrapping any
new surface over its fault

orphic extraction of hollow-
able earth tamed along
a finding grain or double-
cut as foliage re-
members its ruts

curvilinear trenches abide its
erasures until driven to a
crash-cradle made plainly
the trees' at one fitting

Latterly whose world would switch out the site of its hole through picking at gaps in the lattice at home within an obstructed interval but swept out as eye the reflector channel (hollowly) stays on because soundly roomed over, kept for re-entering by other trials of means this local centreless reburrowing into assailments of sonically unmatched recovery a mute enclosure vibrating in trees towards the few derived rentals picking up unowned sounds of a hollow towards

In this hollow projected as inhabiting the frugality of dead space now redistanced by an active scarcity of the living   root lineage along stone crinkle systems   relief profile gives eminent trees from hollows   how the clumps advance by asymmetry-flounces off the vertical   what is outwardly loss is no longer a dent in surface possession but inferential coating put to deference in vest at a layer of offering towards such impaled tapering   tapped out of negative anchorage once caught abroad by its tips

exported grounds of themselves won't
declare a hollow but need
treadings of foliage to aspire
their reparative thin acre

a greened-up pocket pulled
hollow-direct, as saturates
fail but last such
masting cloudward

where the trees become
own code as stricken for-
ward to adhesion, the
vaster flimsy envelope

There is no unfree concave given its nil resemblance to tree   placing a shallow chasm stubbled less by enriching its assembly than commonly de-niching its reticence   a bowl out of its prior scarcity rehung to a differently given-out   becoming a tree-prowl of recession but what this gives of tree masts accordingly the stabs they inherit

Natural resources freed (extracted) from their own local peaks deemed once more immediate ascendancy, an offer of spirit minus forward packs for projection   this is how trees must propagate, resuming a hollow from the presage of itself minus protection

tree cumulus offers the
filter a highly weak
conversion of
removal below surface

if this *is* abscess it won't
drain by trees, may pan its
enclave onto a first
hollow just as the panicked
seed-cloud crowds in

masses of sandless
crescents without solar
safety where even
stubborn lesions
are diffident

swathing the hollow
for its own (reversible)
bulge, filling it out
by exuding from
glands to indicate
pertinent dust is
tree blossom

Young whips wheel the blank weeping into circuits of overhead trouble of place   such tolerant gusting filigrees of rubble   without issue but not as any dead-sending into tree, into what is an aligned integument —what stones do to trees is how trees have done with the gravels of horizon   each is flushed abrasively upon the other as mirrored (tethered to span) in the hollow itself

3: (bowl / trees / dome)

How a co-venture (sting of vacuity, prick of trees) installed its canopy stratus of rootable figments but penultimate in capsule-offering which takes leaf only a single depth away from porch of sky whose branches are a lull from cranking in gulf a hollow spent-away regroups the victim virtues of sacrifrontal woodland tendrils curl apart a resnared dome of green above spare desertion even lacking how these haggards lurk but abrasives in shoot enough for weakly vertical insertion

a branch acrostic
quips absent nervures
of a lost ground's
vertical striation
it might openly
respite its narrows
the tallest way

ascent's no longer
concise surface
new plaiding over
any root-slate
within hollow

occlusive retrievals
steal every mid-
texture set before
mine unprovisional
open sky, now a
content of perfect
removal regains
a stone hovering

Positioned void granted a crackle of exposure reknit by that tactical admission onto whose severals new separable skin marks a shedding that is all for taller sides of the lengths of itself no longer laterally contained the deviation has to be trunk-specific as trained on the sky's own untouchables never any further than a tip's suffered unbowing

Where hollow begins to tumble through its bin of concessions, branch convection tepid enough for infill   waging recovery aisles until its scoop is bundled in with passage towards some unhurting skimpily roofed—not without limp hurtles to sphere where an apparent leavening presses on it   abashed sky could no longer dash this filmiest sheen of depth onto any downward retention   that trees might saddle any green rubble to such pallid gaps

greasing the tangle-norm
sliding a thicket
where it bunches and
indurates, consent begins the
abrogation-caps of
justified crown

wedged trees in-
solvent uppermost
speed their knapped alarms
in fate, within gear
to wait on such
vertical relapses
from entrapment

With trees backing a random tilth there could only be vertical remuneration   light sanding at the lean from branch dries out in valid coast of crest applied sky   doesn't regale a lost surface but pillories it, poles towards its refluct stand, then riffles over according to gleanable cravings of sky   the original quarry bowl didn't know its own swerve but at this soldered vacuum is in lieu of that exact suction of extraction

What sinks any prospecting beech onto new embedding   it lives out of cavities which can't be what interior it is   untethereds of confined diversity   tread gaps of upshot into what it is not   leaving off traipses the stakes of dropped traffic *onto* sky   any affinity between intent and container is long since better removable upon slims of an upright condition

englobing some motes
finds hollowness
coaxing the trees

fixed leaching onto
feedables of sky, a
prism of tinctures
filtering off this
bottoming reflex,
a prison tree starved
into radials

never ownmost
scoured to exposure
but insofar
sown hoist = canopy

which allowance kicks
back as will maim
at sky, never less be-
hind its evens each
way the punches
into gauze beset
with crumple-zone

Foliages as a musk of secondary detention thronging right across the directional span of recomplied flow   diagonal giving out at taper from which there is no tertiary abstention from an unaffordable pool of sky   the hollow's own flare is now primary propension   these trees put up a baffle against clean mirroring   invite from hollow skies whichever eye to eye is steady refraction but weaker cross-defensive lash   petty offering might follow out a tie of co-figuration, skimped rank blanket taken to vertical image

A co-salience of sluggish hollow protrudes a guided dome *above* trees given that both have these furtherances to go twin taxings conduce to a local vertical, outright lack-stretching to where the true reflect of hollow is unassimilated shelf, self-unsimilars but preparing not to camp their squats on difference unbelonging is original misgiven hole in serious low laps hollow-noosed across averted skies which are becoming attentive to so much arboreal dilution

whose own plurals
regroup at a petulance
of horizon, what
will settle on
uncorrected woodland
done to dome

no infill prescience
other than setting
stubs to growth
amid nil-contact
attirements above

a bud puts tallness
the other side of
stark entanglings:
the trough itself
is not endless as
might procure
ejectives

forgetting-seeds mirror
swept into safe
barrage until its silo
had transferred
among recall simples
berried in wood community

A plea to the scooped ancestry of ascending with origin to submit fidelity to a forestalled (recelled) compress of ascent this continuity will proceed by way of certain pre-rippages extractable from itself but reshadowable not by itself in the soiled stalls how quarry deflections take to beakier crown summit their own saved as transported remit to emergent shavings

Scarce ration of propulsive allowance   from hole to hollow of its desert ratio of scars, rods of non-compliance insert their repose in sharpness— from any emergence than their steeper smarting up the silent vertical trace   thin-tree upsurge in a tissue of value surfaces skimps its frontage off the unreskinnable   the floor at last has gone post-violation, letting its sediment obtain in tall accretions

packing infill amid missing
tackle of a vertical screen
already denuded by what
they have been but
stiffly green-out fliers
of what they have seen

abandonment kicks up a
foliage zest, ankles
woody enough for re-
suming the nest
in skies of dis-
similar redundancy

sprawl the assailment
below ground without
lodging ground again, trees
crabbily baled it out
to needfuls of sky

A well-damaged forest of origin but here impoverished enough over trucked ground to add ribs to a dome of surface   the sky at carriage lies across a quarry's taciturn infill of swerve from applied curve   once so hollowed-amid not even whichever horizon has risen from this tuft-haze will need any bushier phase of arrival   export a ground in sequence (of loss) then follow it out in stolid trans-arboration   how the sky nerve is now free from further amplification

Postprudent which is replicable branchwork   exchanging clouds of foliage for lanceolate flanges   with border issues over such as this sky's inadmission under outlet   how a hollow files itself forward from the unsheltered dome above   transmittance through an alleviated rancour of leaves relives odd feathers some way before the flutter of sky: from very slightness an inference trusting to uprise deprived of twist   on the same meagre footings paled into sky as tree particulates   it stirs faint realms of axiomatic greenery

this hole once followed out
by soft invasion
a bracket on scant
worlds not listing
but where a least diagonal
researches above

brightness along branches
stabilising the skyward
occupancy, a further
minute population filter-
ing the vertical-among

encroaches on pit-
iful lances of return
to where they have
given their practiced
ascendant apparitives

Feel tall happenings of those that wouldn't have abstained   cleared spoil within a landtrap towards its focus abroad, above newly pliant remote (unremoved) contours: a swab of expired stone grits throughout its grainmost   what transpires from a blot of allo-receptive plain sky: sinews of emergency relation in direct funnel of subtraction   never without the hollow retort pincered on some tangential float between fabrics

The satellite a hollow benorms once the gleam is tree retinal, a dish newly lagged on reply   as such severed twice over but diagranular enough to reseed its ceilinged surface *upon* sky   missing ground (massed on uses) will meditate (secondary residue) in offerable tertiary tremble   once a bundle of trees does ladle its detachment through ownership of slab provisions of steer   resolve whole cities onto segments before facing again how forest plugs will stop up cubicles vacated by displaced provision, the other stone facade

a last glut of injury
reads steady shaft to
ground, diminished for
vertical, but this
places close shift

traverse a retrait
but up vertical layers
swivelling out
horizon-from
the unfillable

co-fetchings above
tails of trees
such an active scut
of absence stripes locals
off waste, asymmetric
rust *in* sky given
a hue of the cycle

Trees no longer silently pitted towards hollow   the whole reflectance goes truant outschooling its tools   at least two beds ahead of sky   can there be secondary contours beside these non-originals, just slighted primary to be scouring?   themselves not below location but from where the sky is a mere homotone of conciliance   even where these verticals assent to its tertiary difference?   a near-apparent vertically sought, eclectic proximity by way of blatant horizons thrown through tree   actual not only what is but standing the offer from

The quarry as frontier reduct this side of   the negative tarries the bar but sieves its secondary trees direct on verticals   these petty unconditionals settle horizon to abut (disavow) a scoured contrition   shimmer a rigidity amplified across trials of leaves   the vertical reference is on trail but dissipates around the nub of any offering point   except the hollow had already affected what as nexus will no longer remain bare to become a shell owing (shallowing) its very allowance of vertical advice

no trees had ever
trudged sky, do
allow hollow re-
fringed eyelets to
be squinted onto it

the sky ahead of a
tree's head, what growth
there is from within
eroded past a rinsing
tendency forwarded
from tandemly
abandoned footings

taken such back-
stoops unlocking a
cellular at birth, sky
narrows to a tunnel
of outsize green
deceleration

An impenetrable has been lightly subtracted here   until such rogue mattering beneath the patina of world is put to its rising porosity of the slightly anchored   absorbent but still slim as the slip leaves will give to trees   by which beech, oak and hazel confessed their portions of calm liable for staid sifting but here not rationed to their sliver of conferring a tallness-from   still foregathering piecemeal at a sky-set   self-negating a present given but leanly as gift *to* gift   a nothing-before less its emerged faction on behalf of

Not that disaccumulation is such but that its accompaniment can be enfolded   given to a horizontally dipped placement already gone with—might staringly behave a tangent's elsewhere local to the vertical verges on stem   the one sky array there is that trees could only be pushed so far—reposable affinities not to be rushed from their waste tassel, speculative lankness of accord   the vertical *is* naked safety but craves to be mediated under whips of cover

emplacement slid down
gullies until a future gift-
residue breathes them
a tab of height, what
terrain hasn't arrived to
but patiently riffles
their infill-trees
of the galleyed updraught

a green cloud of exit
from niche will clarify
skies offered more than
a respite from release,
scarifies exactly
the original drop-relief

minimally out of time
within this breadth, no
stepping up the space
either side but micro-
clefts for acorn and mast
to re-endure their cramp-
compliance, tenuous
clint of affiance

Not goading own stones dropped below nakedness   and only now brittly skirting such prone overtakings at the flaps of trees   some temporary membranes leave themselves more than a pruned shelter   trans-lateral remound of empty surface confesses solvent slightnesses about sky which are no longer any depletion on the flat   trees swell from hollow to bulb pouting uplift itself   a chambering climb never without stalk, what bettering skies have no disguises before

Any roundness of desertion transmits   not now frittering its stems but leaves a supplement's emergency belonging already slanted into change the ravages of relation   whose skies in the midst of such an exaction were enough   the common tissue by which we are offerable, scarcer even than additive void making good as local slenderness   or a counter-attrition taken away with what cones its stay beside a tapered tallness in a continuable out-of-means, so intent on allowing hollow to replenish dome   more than a marked damage-lapse but with further lip in the sub-round of offer   what is supposed to appear needs arborial tedium, the active revenue of a hollow

edge of throw-back
in pit into which
belated junctions of
trees are a membrane
lifting the silence

how we are guided
from sortal deprivation
to an additional dent
in the intra-vertical
an echo of absence
promised a cropped
para-void towards

therapeutic renegades
of belonging taller, in-
verse scope of the lat-
est famish of dust,
vertical sediment
is early dropped stick
a comb to the barrage
available to prop

At a void closed, to the earth still further beneath it   such does no-hole-like openness to sky if not remitted through an instep of bowl compactly devoided of the untoward, a vagrant implantation on behalf-of —vortical implication towards one fraction of another's gyrating the alls of it   conditions spill minimal locations of the unconditional   trees of such boarding particulars forming the threads of a vertical natural history

What is an outer side of the pitted-out   how do these assault trees
push a fold of fielding its hollow towards tokens of horizon?   not
so much a pellicle between but an intermediate faction   which offers
on (vertically) their own variant convexity   unlateral compaction is a
hole new crossed   ramified by stretching a nothing-of   tree targets are
communal sectaries from within the scarce-toward, gently translate   a
nothing for too long dis-stoned but sufficiently convertible through its
dimensional remonstrance, a wood-throat's cratering pivot   inner/outer
horizon no entering other than this offerable (*ie* post-open) sparsity

hollow reflector (less
any ground flash)
like a naked eye
must be pocked (pricked),
stalked, stick at
coping for the
mottled gaze

a tissue confides them
flush from leaf to
leaf run out by en-
capsulation to shrubby
envelopments broach-
ing a sky on field

initial multiple cramp-
in towards rarer
limits of ramp-out
always unrapidly wins
the within-tree con-
sent after rasp

If a crater were outlived forever it would still borrow this blister scope of
tree against faults of sky out hunting for it   another order of spreading
ends of vault-height, after-fractures   or their full unpurchased knock
against minute elation   hastens dipped cowl or a cell dropped too
foreshortened for emptiness   seclusion off its spates of thinner, rimless
infill   no additional skies but a modest addiction in sheltering   stone
shivered over towards offerable cone

Trees Not Tending Leaves

2013

but for life we'll not be rid
    of the leaved fossils
Elizabeth Bishop

...and thus lets the covering rise as such
Martin Heidegger

trees not tending leaves   marking a fond shaft with their elision:
veins ply back to trunk   apply to saturation at bark level

buds hire only to the bulk of root   transpiring reversals of
leaves   is there any turntable foliage of diremption, some
internalised rubble of planar thickening?

every leaf given to hardspore of shelter   source begins once
terminus probes an unwieldy stripe of tendency

leaves not a way in but a grace of tackle beyond stalk, to
stick with tree-plaiting

a rifled woodiness shaken by what there is to blow out a tip   leaves
have no alignments not their passage (to and fro) attachment   a
kernel flickering a tangent

emulate what squats from mass on a tree's leaves
because tree-roots are narrow flared, speared to a
fluttering across any transferable spire

full to the aisle of branches, leaves breathe-in unchested   not
fringed but ranged in coils   counter-tuned to be sheer leaf at
handling   a tablet of micro-weather

packs a sharp gavel at branch, ingests a knock against
easily grated nil absorption   whose powder this becomes
the leaf of

chaos reads back to outline but a leaf-ful doesn't blank out
any stripped rind of tree

paddled by flaps of shrinkage, the senior thinness given
onto leaf   at rank of no inversion to source but peripheral
conversion of canopy

a leaf-point from which roots no longer charge curtailment
such tabs blunt on flutter-zone no longer postpone
attachment

play out an opaque nutrient film towards drop-point
where its blains dart past every path to us   the
crowd-over is obsolete articulation branch-coked but
sticky with source

mind long woods, nature stood up to the man micro-
shuttered   this fields hope, the old nearest among now

unrotating green moved even sky, every beneath silent
among live trenches of passage, its actual resolutions
suspended which were also branches at leaf-plug   to be
mourned in blocks of tender prong

furled and then myriad-foiled throughout the system, leaf-
cowered boxes deliberately jabbed onto taper, delicately
robbed into spread

a spindle of tree rifles the torpor from leaf   wider
prowess of the straightest sapling

that leaves are a ferment to hide yet never amount to any
skin unsealed   such micro-solo repetitions not in rift of
but off flail of cape

where leaf unravels it won't untie any relief from direct
staples of green retreat   the attachment plight broadens
beyond flotation   thick surfaces are a plateau of
revisionary tree intending horizontal armature

each threatened leaf sub-tubular but not quit of its
stable ballast amid the roll of vessel

the stir of the wild is endlessly pushed leafward, to a taut
unpractised stringing up of puny retrievals

to offer this first rule of alarm to itself   a tree is
only tall of its ruinous leafage, rafters gleaning
up any rigidity and once unfolded never off the
vertical plane

keep this a chosen sheaf, factions verge on rod, ply leaf its
extant range   trees not tending leaves: leaves giving out
trees

radiance so edgy as un-irradiated but tending to
it exactly   until some better air fits panoply to
trees, better to sift winds from their settings of
leaves

behind each hazel leaf a rear shoot overtakes with adjunct
limb of the spray, asymmetric but reading evenly the clips
between shadows

where no bough is wrested from leaf a whole tree
recommences   for leaf this is not wandering but longest
propulsion   taps of branch, clots of leaf   both are tips of
root in no other avoidance

every resin of bunch is recorded in single strands of light,
the bounce no longer derived from branch

to give (ungrieve) likenesses of: terminal strafe freely, not
unwilling to coincide with extreme outer staffing:
experimental symmetry of a tree reduced to one move at a
time, stood at adjacently entwine   spread the uneven
selection a little longer limp with margin

leaf seals at a width of unsortedness, wherever there is
loose brushing at back of twig

trees amid screen, no screening *off* tree in the milieu of its
sublucence: attract leaves to their shallow fords of light

offering round another curl of compressed abandonment
but where detachability gets spent into the burden

any leaf reserve is effectual decodings but whose
departures are dragged over an entire tree towards
forward canopy

the mild randoms of shelter are towards drawn
descenders: each tail of leaf a siphoning off sheen
losable allusion to main (though coolant) body of tree

the forest nothing but transparencies below, a whole
leafage folded into waiting on new studdings from above

a dart of shirt shadow, what rips in shifts, towards
covering what cannot be thrown over

once canopy, leaf initiative traps its way back to source
across wavelets of unprimed shelter injects new
obstructions   the taunt goes intent across fresh
cancellations of tree

the great haven of shelter commotion, this tact of life and
its supported toss   off assentive edge

raggedly above root retrenchments but never fallen except
full against exposure

with leaves only spent to take effect, what is put upon tree
in its flight from naked originals

how leaves crimp into trees a counter-nape of repletion
coating the shadows inward from a mantle of relief but at
direct stressed dark   a skin of trees declares leafage
unstonily   pack roots in scree and then guess in film
pressed out on flints of leaf brittle enough to flash over
what a scrapped flank occurs to

throwing into lean system, these infinitesimals put throat
to tree   aligned with bracketing from a peripheral canister
inwards   from which cloud stanchions occlude, grates
origin through every sheddable fixative on tree

where the insensate struts are, how featly, leaf provokes
dead-spate of tree

at a rate unsparkling placids of support do have
seeking not to bind its speckle-ratio but from its weight
of compound slightness

encompasses all main loops of tree   these micro-tassels
quaked from shape towards flatness of root

easily leaf knows it can't bounce its way round circuit
at the same motionable rub   investing its
sliver (post-quickened) at a ramp stacking for trees:
a diaphragm redolent with lignin trust but
prone to a further drape-indexical elasticity

nothing flimsy withheld in forest, the weakest is strong-
collared in leaves   little enough ground *beside* woods
than what is already beneath a precedent of leaf

not so much extensive intake along jointure as position
sessions of leaves

normal trappings of signals of light towards a mass flicker
of spectrum   then caught dropping equally, packets
offering their fluctuation zones   mantle is frantic petal
enough for unflowering crust

the rotation of fragility feathery for blanket of tree
micro-signal of leaf but in no close-circuit waverings   the
crest of the cull bodes a broader overlap of root

once out of branch whatever takes lackings off proper
stem   shorn of leaf is shown central unassisted roof of,
the departure given to

that leaf allusively rusts to core

onto this nest of branch-horn the single pommel of bud in
dome   allayed at once by leaf done

infestation to own leaf-order, that people are now the
science of the park   how root makes increment from
what surfaces of disadvantage assort

heaving over root-steer, so many leaves to have been
stripped on form, they are not the reprisal but the retro-
sags of design, where alignment puts them ahead of itself

displacement cut to leaf only to envy a lightened origin to
this siphonable intent   trees rebegin here, not at offering a
duplicate sprig but at the leaves' own myriad tubulars

a canopy pulls itself up onto the shallows   from which any
larger proffering may combine with the hardstanding it has
retracted onto   not structurally but out of care of a mass
terminal flutter

tresses gained each day across slight incline of trunkal
vein

not tended because pure relief of shelter dissolved to
catchment and without any skin of it desiring the trees'
advancement

untentative separables out of a rash of gummy leaf at
drop-point   the deep pitching into tree posture   where
abandonment is its moundal and the stubble of loss evenly
recessive

whose leaf-production inclines to no crop and whose
distribution of cast-offs pervades what is previous of
shortened limb in tree

not lenient in leaf but a cusp fluid, the curve of any slight
ontological retainment strip by strip, not least of any static
if staring into its own unobstructed scatter

leaves flow to the core of what doesn't go with them, the
apex was a nurture untended at its slightened-erect:
intends debaseable vertical offering, all equation though
scarcely any inclusion

a tree alone with its dead propulsion along shaft once out
of leaf

relinquishing the ribs of tree but never its hoop
speculative immensity out of a previously thieving system

love the tree but be at bay outside it   defect onto its tinge
of touchy aggregation   a reflex of unshuffled steepness
and not a limb   among it

a filter rubble baling out trees but dried to its vegetative
plane of momentarily tethered elongation

the prophetic frame brittle enough to overleaf itself, the
slightness takes that ontological vetting into net

slurs are the leaf amount towards woods   to fore-tie an
eclipse of any solo depth brushward   so flat at thread

these extreme lintels of surface   lenses flushing off
intemperate core delay

leaves prolong, in failing, any ride along curve of the
diminishment, hipless leaf set *to* hip   by choice of a
descendent (root-purge) array   the turning airs of the
darkening sheaf

settlement stride now disclosing a rammed condition   in
at the leaf and proposing veterate ramification through the
pore

if leaf profile drew into tree it was no longer a summary
envelope   at drop-time the immaculate fritter is a shutter,
ie the click towards season, the roller armature off branch
delivery

leaf-cowl? but less any towelling, why be hooded to a pin
of tree precinct?

unbestrewable hinterland at the root-well itself   what
leaves are covering here is how ground hovers

what is window to leaf is a shadow to tree

the sender nervure, communitarian leap reckoned token
arch, staple breach

casting a fingerable spell through the arm, the
harmlessness of heavy to root

there may be tacit reserves of leaves but no substrata   all
layering is towards light suckles along a trial of minimally
anchored deposits   opposition drawn (to root) but already
thawing at a latitude of surface

a compaction of the local at its real space deep root   a
lyric life rattling off stem   dried to a vertical vegetative
immersion

partition only along peculiar planes of adjustment   how
a toll of tree flies to its neighbour connection, on every
leaf of collision

if tree is what petrifies on its stand, the haze of leafage
was even earlier than resuscitation onto trivial sill

lengthening the immateriality of diaphanous sewing,
seams accrete veins, display spares for credentials of
concrete wing, tree at its filmiest span

leafings not so much in trans-ascension as condensers of
soft shield towards a target at the drape of rise

leave it to leaf level to flatten out the condensation   a lair
of tree nursed into leaf, hung there from finer hairs of its
concealment lap, trunk to disc of random depth

what is lent out is for a time worthless in leaves   leaf out
of leaf, done with branching off some wry platform terror

the trees' self-handling of a girth of earth

insular but leafed over onto the thud of defection   foiling
all tenderness as though itself a soil, the seal's rim at this
several of flap just out

with leaves on scrap, to afford what the bark ratio scarps
verticaled towards

leafage is a concision of origin but no reversal, scathing
opposite traversal at such a lean fillip of beginning

this tending to finitives is not for coaching leaves, render
them their apprehending lapse of the cult of themselves:
not boughs freshen them but the whole blunder of tree

the knack of lift through branches not green in their own
weight   how the unplenty fails its forest onto leaves of
acquisition

that trees are clotted to leaf-synthetic mutual contusion:
only then the trip-circuits become root systemic,
accelerated reserves

dendritic alcoves hedged in leaves   to compete with
forest petrified under its own shingle

leaves diverge so that no tree-shift is hunched along stem,
resorting prematurely to shaft from a columnar decrease
of root   it takes a treeful to let go, into a season of ground
reclusion

five leaves to a sprig rotate root in prolific sparseness
they are the remissive adjunct to any turbine trumped in
shaft

stab tendency (spiritual staff) moves tree into its prime
stiffness before sunlight   leaf tendency waits to grow the
plane of it, a furniture of lentils at risk of the horizontal

any motion from stem needs to give leaf its upper hand, its
ulterior passing from hold

stem undeflects a light-beam as what leaf assigns to a
complexity of reception   the only totality is the tendency
to shredding, counter-filling, retro-grounding

gleamed with leaves invites a passenger array, the main
transition force an expansion of direction siphoned off
roots once lean targets are all about them

careless leaf tendency to over-report capacity across a grid
of root and unlock loose bars of branch in the enticement

emissivity of leaves tendoned along blackbody of refill
root   any enclave is restored its tipping place along an
exact mediation of planes

tree bitten into by its contorted amounts at shaft but then
wrapped over by the easing levels of leaf

a leaf is no more than a fan toward veins

leaf-tip rolls back but only to compared zones

not probable than an oak comes scarce to leaf?   there
lean protraction had another function, to insert/centre one
shave of itself before bluntness learns the like   any galled
becoming into blatant quarters?

leaf is beyond making for horizon but risks further
demarcations down its nervure to set a trunk to it

garrulous reckoning among young leaves or a toll of root
shiftlessness   a town of leaf upon a tuft of tree

is there any stretch in the forest, or the sound of leaves
proving it? do webs of leaves get crustal amid the trees'
dark options?

behind any leaf-film a thickness-room of bark   how the
back of leaf projects a temporary span across what carries
a lintel into wood, becoming the tree's foreground desertion

if there is a twisted fern of leaf, it is not as resembling
erosion that it will sprain through to tree

floaters at a rise of unsifted tree, but one root for the
levities of it   scoured to the ridge of airstream   a
lipsidedness in tongues of leaves   never aloof, gaudily
bitten onto stem

as light is absorbed onto wafers of co-penetrant shade
puts a saddle on tree, what it rears up to

voiding the eventual pallor of axes, leaves desiccate to
their own letting be cleared

leaf quota with its special mark in the least and lightly no
quittance from forest enclave taunting its snipe of foliage

oak boughs zoning over momentary (seasonal) ligament
or, walk a periphery across droplets from the oak's
undiscardant root

how bark itself will shade fugitive leaves once fallen on
primary root cradle

agile asperities of departure but no anti-flare over a mask
of fallen green   ex-leafage but not reducing tree to tusk
against owning a post-nurture

trees thinly peopled as forest but knowingly towards a
leaf's emigration

leaves erring only so far as chips of breeze, then a feasibly
notched unsteadiness

to fling the span of trees across their flattest heel   what is
probed for plane listens for a monotony of root beneath its
levelled real

torn fore-cores splashed across acrids of delivered trunk

essential graft from thin foil   untilled seams of leaf

slight (confirmed) basis for thickening forest after a
depression of leaves   as mesh is to haze that spills
glistenings from runnel and will leave trees to their wooden gauze

what is it in trees that will abandon this unguiding
supplement but be inflected by it, as far as every residue
of future root and branch?

so that neither branch nor trunk risk a false middle,
dispensible leaf keeps within the weave of root   baseless
but grounding the overtones of growth

> kindness comes from repairs to vicinage alongside, leaves
> in addition to thronging branch

a standard of leaf now drowned off root but holding to
gale of tree

> though leaves relapse to an unhumped nod at root they
> forage no after-bush   what is stealth of root without a
> matching ditch of leaves?

not punching to foliage but parching any false relay in
canopy   a milder earth will thicken off the stalk

> what is neglected at keen branch is uncancelled whenever
> it falls to leaf

trees advise woods but leaf *provides* unsolitary tree

> bark more losable than leaf but lesser in the scales of
> looseness   a canopy will strip away at any uncandid
> symmetry of dissolution

shells of a dicing myriad not diving for tree but drawn to
creeping root   through a given fall that is first rehearsed
peripherally

a motley of attachment to be least kindred at this anchor
place is a speculative commonplace

if I could target a leaf I could break a tree   each lack to its
full quota now steering the assembly

loaning and shafting, the pressure of injured plane
growth is needled but its extenuation can only be
published in a leaf abroad

layers of it could be called no second leaf once there is a
crucible of root to infiltrate

leaves not spikes but spools of freshness   what must be
proved off-role around a stone of root

contractile slippage but only where shrivelled leaves
concur with vanished root

not just a rind that can be plucked but a wallow of tree
shirked into root   as every leaf will batten against the
grain of tree but not shut the spectrum out

all restitution must be unsheathed, baseless, in this nearing
to root

as a trunk is to be without roots unless impelled into leaf
by which a canopy sails to the cull (corralled into scanting
the onslaught of origin)

to code departure for origin but disarray the fall   leaves
proven to allay the annual upgrade on girth

the obstructive sower of an unbereft   where a fed leaf
fell, it tested the allowance of it

forest on forest decompressed over grass cropping root,
steps set upon a stroke of leaf

first seen *above* the woods   what but a leaf gesture?

thick woods make do with a rim of prime truth   a radiance
dropping into leaf   at a gamut of fall

fallow leaves or spun too few to rest among none

whose branches fling from the no-tree pinched out on leaf
touched at variable remaining   nothing serries against
leaf, not even relief from tree

scarce of leaf to be unhardened at the nub

loss of leaf is not lack of leaf but the main shower of
implication   a spate of retention grounded in jettison

a degree of leaf history: not peeling but falling, not
sedimenting but stirring the retro-gears of origin, to dip
periphery to incentive   captioning around root a freckled
regularity not yet its own

what is staled just above root level packs a tree's spire, a
race towards crust of assembly risk

who chills the leaves can't farm the roots   leaves daren't
practice own lattice but do intend to revert from loose
gathering to generative tourniquet   withdrawn a whole
splint through vertical tree

new leaves mildly ahead of main tree armature   not just as
filter but meek exculcation of infra-erectional forest gain

fall of leaf less a defacement than juxtaposition of forest
ambition   cyclic interruptions but depicting surplus in
its mode towards minimal core   as surrenderable
undiminished but glancing offside the range of whole-tree
shrivel

hurt at an attendant particle gives release from hollow
centre but forwards a relation scarcity active at the core of
allowance   that leaves hang *in* the hollow if feeding its
light onto a texture of dumped reception   undappled
remission to forest tree   fleeting post-flotation but applied

dwindling off stem but still not stammering event
compaction towards outfill, emissive tab bio-upgrading
the goal of fuel

an estimate (right through the diaphragm of tree) via
extimate (sentry) confluence whose calculation-rate is
permuting at a now negligible peripheral loading

the rind leaps to its co-plummet rest, as plunge is obliging
an arc of tree   there's more than just one binding
(gliding) to estate

if leaves subside once unhooked out of air they concrete
themselves unlocked onto the logic of tree diameter as
negotiable post-securities of perimeter rapture

structural revision pitches its sheddings through a
composite noose   untended towards but fully received at
any horizontal so induced   give the forest a suddenness
of ulterior cladding

blunt elevation of entire tree towards wind profile:
shaped by what trivial summons offers detail in
community (plus/minus the commons of leaf)

that leaves might be not just extenuating but penetrative:
weak local contests onto the driving hub of tree: roaming
earthwards their own zoning beside para-root

cycloid occlusion   once leaves are turned off they print
another system's breadth   another horizon fronting on
incoming forest foot

that the veil is cloven inheres canopy at meta-dispersal or
distressed particulates *dress* mutant attachment, separated
stems bow jointure-specific   dia-semination via
enscarced deference of fall

praying
// firs \\

attenuate

2014

Une chose ressentie naïvement comme bonne, amicable, à cause de l'attenuation, dans ce reflet, de l'autre lumière qu'on ne peut regarder en face

Philippe Jaccottet

Think of ten quiet trees with their nerves in the air

Alice Oswald

Yes, since the trees
bear a double cone

Ed Dorn

I

firs in faith   of angularity ingrained

firs in case   of singularity arrayed

firs at base   a seedling tethers

firs at praise   enlaced alike hazard

greenbone sour to needle
lean spark of a neighbour
or lenient taperings
more lately subcandescent

entails the full table effect
at no accessory (ascendant) root
as in least cancellation of height

prayer not like a fir, no
forsaking any one of them

how to plant prayer on its
raked scope, offer a leap
from rampant sediment, what
will become a neck of fir

pro-plantational not in
solitary planted faction
and so conceding prayer

it isn't virgin forest
pleads origin
but conifer stands
ripened to alienation
heeding their
intemperate spires

connect the rash at unfelled tops
a sighing norm of prayer

less to serve at tree than
send it about its comparison

that void is compromised by
sensory declension, so far
slightened over prayer
the tension of unincluded
things aligning with no
gradient but orison

desire to add a grain of falling
short to more of the earth's
this is already prayer's
probative store

every prayer
alternates between
fir clear of fir
without contending
any substitution

staked for no lack but in
post-redundant savour
an under-grain of the

given exposed to a whim
of the same, free of its
own graft of otherings

to flood a poverty along
the vein of its scarcity
until tall commonality
is no longer sparse
but fellow continuance

trees it assumes had their own
purity or peak origin but
not an inclusive poverty of
attendance: praying beside
needs no taking aside

among the unpleading branches
I hear refrains of my soliloquy
spare density of among

can the firs deliver new keys
to requite the compression of
seed? their explicit cone
is vertical, ex-spherical

what is upright is gift-
apparent but not as prayer
a sample of transparency

so that green shoots
in season don't inhibit
the stubbed proclivity
of horizon   strew needles
year round at this para-
recessive admission

most a givenness
but less in givingness
pulled through knots
of branch exception
quite given-over to a
with beyond withinness

tapered impassivity
reclining at the least
ripe effort of gift

the order of love commits con-
tingency, remission towards
cares a sparseness, for
what is beggared rears up

a greeter is more than
the whole, we smart
in the common alls

transfer the known to the
sown in place of, to be
prayed not at a
shadow of prayer's poverty
but already expressive
in the shadow

at the foot of firs
in unstolen time with
a parting guide

a prayer lasting out its
cycle, fasting before the
seasonless rejoinder of fir

radial in its shaking out
horizon, not paring it
before dawn, *this* clean pleat
is not *that* vertical

praying firs to the
attenuate ample
of their office

not feeding off a conspectus
of disaster, what was sown
in blank cell gives to hollow-
ness its own arisen stem

prayer at its treeless
frequency, a vow sturdily
stripped of nothing else
and the tree in position

a field whose postures
are open to those who
don't obsess their own

owing prayer its stem
or a localized bent?
a swaying attachment
handier than a wave?

not so much an ad-
junct as a counter-
coincidence, still teeming
with what is no better
sacrilege in tree

given-to will have exhausted
the objects but not the
rugous implicity of shelter

a fir's rooted saturation
counter-active specialist
attrition at the break-out
of vertically stable form

in spate of untamed ful-
fillments where distance
resorts short, bidden attract
arrival beyond reach

II

Shelter variegates over an already curdled nakedness   aspiring attainment patches a lattice of attachment   whichever over-green boughs have been crowding the slant: precarious homing but not competing with the *precor*   the earth is also a privatory language not yet debarring the rareness of its concurrence

Difference's unrivalry sets the firs swaying at branchwork   stylized conifers not so much close-grown as an alibi for narrow fold-out (tallness)   if upward then a prayer-flaw at the hemming

what is diminutive
    is transitively disclosed
    no sect in prayer than
    across ascendant surfaces

    light towards apex
    once hatched in prayer

light hooking climax
    since fetched through fir

Stations of shelter, rations of prayer per attenuated stanchion of report, the co-consistent of pared ballast in tree   accessible clearing to a contemplative barrier of place now perforate with firs   the rippling laterals of tree cover, pining turbulence of a glade's worth of prayer, occasional grade of observant fir

not reciprocal parity
    this intimacy of disparate
    emergence, an on-behalf
    without latter abandonment

shaggy at the catchment
        but in abstinence
        toward replete
        co-intendance

the paucity of emergence
        overtakes every prayer's
        minute candour of completion
        prior over or beneath
        full precedence horizon

towards that easy constriction
        within-beyond   no phasing
        the midst unless
        with its sediment elements

Overtly in small things become the frequency of scarcities at depth proto-asides *at* the latitude of conifer securing-as   the seclusion of an elective rind in nature   a presage of skin almost synchronising a shaved light   the lack is a conciliatory snaking out of the solitary

is small-scale foliage
        petitionary? is the align-
        ment only slender
        between agreed aptitudes?

don't pray out of a slender-
        ness of evergreen but
        heed its bodily
        emitted attenuation

Firs of no particular invocation put ballast on asymmetric aspiration, thinness *toward* intention, no trace in this adjunct of any preliminary abstention   fractious taper prompter than pulse of ruin   that

prayer sighs up without notice   abiding the slights encumbered in
laddering the faults of beckoning   but not the rearing out of what is
enchambered, chafed green of its silence

a given stem
    mottled in seed but
    packed into its narrows
    the compression of
    prayer's indisposition

the green durance
    of a lull
    in the surmounting

Follows an uplift whose credal slope is not the offering itself but a facticity predicting tilt, instituting a latent proportion   how what is less-than is on vertical budget of collateral inhesion of the thinly tall—here where there is scarcely a ramification but ductile prayer

Tactless presence minimally needling the invisible   thornless in sheer puncture injecting this upbraid of approach   sheltered here for old growth towards a transitional fabric of apprising   having its risk in a yield of capture   into the deprivation of aspiring plight   sieved through prayer more a stitch than a frond   a seam waits to be planted and once in earth otherwise   remaining out of season in all its timely buffetings

it is how conifer caps
    the ridge indiscriminately
    that is dutiful

stem between leaves
    and root, what inhibits
    any shouting down
    of prayer. Leave it to

the blunter casings,
in spruce peg its
needle savour
on shrubby cradle

The conformation flows from a poverty awry but directionally enjoining, sharing the towards of any disquality of emergence   the from-which gently suspending the at-which   the ethical circuit is not reversion but what skims off static insufficiency on-behalf-of

Whence a retired earth gives up its thread in the form of a root gradually untwisting before the pull of the vertical   only direct ascent is quietly taut of its prior bedding

no indoor arboretum
        for this laudant privacy

the onsurge is a
        regimen of fir rife
        around stonier parade

The zonal instincts of heaven and earth, cinctures of firs in the round, the tint of prayer or an attentative perfusion   towards an easy constriction of wherefrom they immure beyond   unphased but lasting in prayer, sediment-elementaries

Let up with the post-brutal not yet delicate green world   prayer one long spathe of it   the one becomes unequally saggy before the other until asymmetry dilates the whole offering   how we in nearing take to some sheathing in reserve at the incline   that firs break the plain view without stabbing it

out of conifer   nothing of
trunk gone naked
solely a shuttered riposte
across peeling
needle-loss confers
a just flatness on ground
amassing sharp
over zonal carpet

A factical exceeding of experience (pared down at the surpassing) not enacted unless pre-offered   not prior to unless according a pincer-delay in firs   to work at a supplement reduced to prayer, untaunted by the whole   not in place of but micro-stiffened (touched) according to
shelterable at the unstraying mishap

any cull in prayer
is already called away
from lulling the
invocation

III

Prayer at its mute case but an apprisal (praise) that traced a containment
of its own unowned   other-than not what is alterity to a world's non-
origin   a gift depleted enough to thin forwards of entire horizon—
probes of givenness without addition but by gift a more-than not
detracting from any slights a reception will have undergone

Pray the "as nothing" of a not nothing of its asides toward promise:
dismantling is not an unsheltering   if dispossessed then its actant
scope companions on behalf-of, there is no *posse* not already greeted
in its shorter grain   meted out in a less-than not going without, no
provisioned comparisons of lack

prayer never has the
trail of what it accepts
but knows it has
postponed nothing
in the grateful
divagation

Goes outside the foreshortening of alongside but without rucking the
close at hand, a fir has narrower unsteadinesses than its horizon, wavers
only from a stick of puny summit   foreground is preliminary then
occlusive   the goad must be packed with finite compression as far as a
vertical release of concession

Pray throughout, pray within, by virtue of a thickly paraded earth   co-
provokes just such quota-assemblies of trees   the final innocence of
over-intended flanks: common prescience to God in paring the world
less any steer of horizon but at swooped plenary in tapering from fir

To prevail over facticity not in any soilless addition   rather, set before
an horizon which clarifies at the non-subtractive slights of it   the bond
has tapered into response so any holding-towards has not ebbed   ready
with the again of silence, praise listens across its violation at a compact
alterity   retrieval is what is winnowed past this asymmetry of co-
possession

scarcity performed at its
    salient degree-
    certainty: how the
    fir in line pro-
    trudes appointment

Self-abandonment blown a soil of relation, rations moving it along the
way of direct sail   its prayer is a peopled fringe to any doing without
    immovable furniture of firs, no blunter storage

adverbial brow of trees
    fronting all this
    condensation: praying a
    conversion-package
    admit placed intention
    to unripe density

Apart from this turning, the world has a treeless agenda   it is to
a blunt earth not an unspindled one firs gave countenance   what
won't be deposed longs for belonging's slender terms, at an offer of
enactment disposable-to   prayer not without modulations according-
that   standing in the midst of unretractive firs but which forward the
granular nearings

relatively lacking but
    more generatively slight
    before an unconditional

living a call forward
of its echo   where
its own effect
tapers into elation

No degree of emptiness in this disincentive, love remains before a
cusp of firs   how bunched between graded voids that they draw their
tincture towards what the etiolation can now conduce   holiness
unstraying so as to be not self-subsistent   no longer monological
within the ricochets of call   likened to the other but below any
bracketing out of conversion not being alike

porous to gesture of
fir insofar as receding
before a limit gives it
groundable projective

A borderlessness adhering to intricate screens, textures of vicinities
emerging   into their inflection of transmit limit to limit   adducive
of any forestalling not bound to its opposite   less than a full terrain go
free extent of a pause/hitch on behalf of

Dismantling of self from an arousal over-mantled   by what is
impenetrable or obstructively near, shelter driven rapt by taper of its
vertical plane   prayer on hold before fir without meaning it a clearness
of harness   guesses across but takes this for patience of circuit   by
which many things can be spared but not revoked

raw insertion can also
be an intercession

prayer of many postures before
fir but one only is prostrate
branch, the one lacking in tier

In bower other than with the firs' own lack of contention   height
foreshortens to reserving swerves of sky   a resentment where scarcity is
unrecouped, attempered in taper   that the sacred cannot appear   that
firs were stricken stable of it   until such impossibles do occur heavily
or lightly   co-slender but intemperate then

        a crucible of collision
                (prayer at fir) known
                even less rampantly
                than the self's sub-
                orned own crux

Prayer takes the flightpath of a world not yet cleared of trees   but
they already betoken its etiolation   the by-tallness of placing ascent to
obtrude through seams already stretching past the flattened way   firs
obsess a periphery beyond what is their focal legion, patrolling a prayer
at its slender successors of margin

to field any reserve before a sieve of exfiltration   how abundant
prayer moves through the brittle shepherding of its texture   its sizing-
at, arising at a common asymmetry of rarities

        awaits a gentler ecology
                of mission at this un-
                ripe upcoding
                of the woods

        do not pray
                in the guise of another
                instilment   let the
                firs be their own
                surplus of salience

        this gives a numinous dis-
                enclosure at the pull of
                newly contingent enclave

Be lessened in world so as not to assuage its brunt taken at the full   let new tallnesses taper with the close-grown of it over every leached place   a spine of outliving become the norm, saddled with already a multiple awakened   least equivalent firs but the prayer-accord has no other junction-weed to put before its equanimity

prayer reposition our non-
    occupation of exception,
    requisition the spare
    place for a lesser portion
    of more inclusive gift

that knots of ill
    attendance become nubs
    of a steadier blockade

what was given
    runs out of apposition
    until admitted again
    at a reproportion
    branching the gam-
    bits of taper

IV

Poverty in the givenness and no longer its scarred retaliation   lets
the tracery go on for an ever   only the scratch of node not its pitch
is annulled by the asymmetry of offerable cone   not an ontological
equality but one uncaused thing granting way because another's
reducible is made out in prayer   the implement falls but the tooled
plantation's deferring-to recurs   a mode still not scarified relational
enough at its stark supplemental

or starker than enough
no other slights than its elational

lateral furls of prayer
where only a staccato
beak of fir
can be its frontal

How a more primordial than intending is lately offered to the co-
enigma of gift   if periphery is a regimen it is how it lightens the
necessary focal contagion but with no other elsewhere than this squat
intimation   an impossible but groupable micro-kernel fulfilling
belief   prayer directed to its thin film wholly outside   betweens of
unknowing not like a lapsed surmise but guided beyond through exact
nodal separations   at each jointure of commonly penetrated shelter

the singularity of firs
an envelope aura
vertically reversed swoop

scalar rapture out of
fluctuations beckon
once trapped to tip

something to be able to hide
givingness among gifts,
another to taper the

refusal of witness
until a vertical tells:
no other shyness
in the rivenness

Faith not safe all the way up   but with its gaps abstaining   crevices attain the hollowed-out of hold until there is no longer a backspill that counter-anchors   any beyond is intimate as this huddles a falling-short —however much the spiralled graze is not a plunge-dissent but still in ascendant torsion

No firgrove but in propelling it   there the bedded streak calls out its supplicatory difference   the nudge of prayer before particulars in tallness

procession of tree-ranks
just above husk
tensile needle through
to the given penetrant

the error of bare intention
finds out until a glove
spools it to tree:
only dedication
in the hand will
thicken into sign

If prayer is immune hesitation uncoppicing fir will feed it prone infections from above   a contractile endemic among verticals opaque-directional but with no other subsidiary   here is a structure of rarity to secure us against the overts of insularity: rarity is woven from more than one exception but each scarce enough for its givens to be smooth slips

Shade no denser than the filaments themselves, it is prayer which might have swollen badly   a sectored trouble of reception   there is somewhere invoked pattern gives which is not up to the firs' gauges but pleads for common measure of the enactment   prayer can remain a calmness unappointed at which firs do flinch   but without entail of an embodied resentment   rarity full muster

prayer with no tangible swarm
    many exchangeable surfaces
    every layer a first to
    laminate a given-to

suddenly arboreal in
    nexus, a window for
    prayer without exit
    the shutters blown wide
    thrash a taper's gust

the small contemplative
    dart flies into anything
    narrowed undynamically
    growth from grace
    to fletched grist

Firs prolong the envelope of folded things that go beyond, whose belonging is this destination addressed to a standstill but slipping through to the here of it   prayer intimate with latent possibilities but as a counter-interiority   the contemplative gear publishes its mesh before fir   permission is fruit of an inner relation, necessarily seedless across needle

frontage tagged below
    offering, ample etiquette
    of springy re-capsulation

if prayer can be sifted
for agency it is
in compensation
for its needle induction

To tackle the non-simples of staying beside tree   guide its negotiable priority not coming through any arrears of texture   that prayer as trans-subjective might also bracket the trans-abjective   in a foliage skewed across season   don't place the firs' reward structure at their caked evergreen however droppable but in the vertical slightness dividing itself with prayer

Prays alone a not aligned alone but in sharp contiguity with vertically collective arousal   in the slenderness proper to each

faced with a
wedge of silence, a
fineal stage of
murmur pinned to fir

an effusion of fir
follows attachable
offering off branch-
tiered concentrates

Prayer not ahead of a hoped-for but on behalf of   speaking into the "foundry" of what is spoken for found   let the coolant be firs, shielding any request cast to a texture alongside   what passes through the shape of fir is not suddenly the adjoining sharpness   nature keeps its tartness upon a soul's work

not led to any
tree choice but a
common stance alterable
at concise planes of greening

enacts something good
  a midst of uncertainty astounding:
  incomposite midst
  prolongs the taper

Fir actual because prayer is its least   ahead of possibles that derive
from this thrift of approach   there is no virtual reminder this far out
any invocation will squarely bristle with appearance   that prayer is
to describe an arc of address   petitionary target beside the unknown
norm of tree pining-direct to assurgencies like the unknowable

Seam of fir correcting any pole towards until the upright snatches
forward its cladding   spiritually aphonic until this allocution recites
arborial graft   but driven onto a frontier sand richly unnaked with
vertical spoil: grounded at trodden tip of fir   this will be to put
human impossibility through the smallest filter   until not draining
firs any further accords to a mutual silent constriction   convection
towards a point of praise as the glistening taper eases its evaporation—
no specialism is mute where dispersion is species-specific around
accustomed pinnacle

to ask out of not being
  origin, suffer that opacity
  sinuously alongside
  so grouping its vital remove

agonic nesting
  brashed to a huddle of:
  slash around vents of
  lift whose side-rubble
  winds the incline

V

That a local shutter (blinked encounter) prefigures fir   duress
unhidden, worn at the cleft of branch   this single shadow never
obdurate by how much shoots ascend domain within their minimals—
dispossessed of any innermost but at the call of it: tapering through
entire tree verticals cell by cell

pray the offer out of
        bracket rolls of un-
        thicketing fir,
        masts kind as the
        whole attenuation

from inward combat
        to no more numbness
        in tree   a leap
        into circuit but
        fronting the occlusion
        overlooks completion
        in fir   clusive but
        looser than any
        *un*thanked infinity

Less a pact with trees than adjacent compliance, a saving induration of
the unexpected   already heard in the woody granular of staking out
the cry   sortals from trees, a self in response heavily unsifted   each
shaft burdens/pardons its vertical delight   twilight wiry enough for
gratitude

accentuation was always sudden
        in firs   seal in speech
        the through-rings of co-
        agular recourse whose
        definition is each
        needle-point escape

Transinternal sparseness, average felling amid unblunted trees   offers
a silence to any geophanous comer beset by vertical contours   firs
become apex-wise sufficiently ahead of their supposed brittle piercing
piece on piece of the interim gift co-adjourned without spurning
jointure as its common ambience   this last composite of prayer onto
the grain, at its addressable than-which

the scarce which seems
to have expected us
never extracted us
leanly inside
this anticipation

our lack of beginning
only rescinded at a
human *tangent*:
the saddled stem
girthed to a tree's
unslippery taper

Where is the stalk of lack in lack itself?   desiring what is already given
(to desire) presents this contraction in approach, a null desiting   held
taut before the decompression's usable stealth in tree

The excessive pristine chastened to a non-frugality   adjacent vacancy
which opens us up to fillings of assistant occupation   greening of loss
(return to the cellular) not to be taken for no vertical organism, leaves
were ascendant in brief   pray the accusative initials of calling just
above zero-from   so affirms any object of adherence/reversal as bodily
response granted its lesser term, the non-economy of scarcity-upon

without secret memories
of my inexplorations
onto the publicity-array
of trees secrete a
candid self-racking

loss let go *to* loss
elongates the plenitude
our own presenced-to
harbouring out
fir-gusted

Excess of pastoral is its first abscess of encounter   if the swirled governor swells to plantation it steers for updrift in fineal sleekness: remission of packed vaulting spreads with another tree in it   if we are told apart it will not specify the wound against   this passive exit toward the unbearable in height of   leaps by fir go across a collage of verticals   that a prenatal intimacy (first to within another's given-from) might also be ontological inauguration   paraglobal in sizing all the littered seconds of devotion

intimacy wide open to
consistent anterior rumour

caught short with some-
thing to offer the un-
adorned   a singularity
denser than its own exception

Silence before a forkless tree is active translation, not a needled decoding   how many silences can there be?   an impure abstention but one pact in conical tree: less clamour than unmuffled sills of outspread   letting oneself be shadowed minute before all cramped measures of shade   thanks to these caps foreshortening, gift will not be solely reabsorbed by its own gifthood

confiding in negations
but just to the point where
unhesitant firs are exempt

reduced gift
sieves through prayer
while retaining
fir for mesh:
enough impurity
to grant all the relations

neither despoiling the
world nor steeping it
in its own acid wilderness

VI

Here a prayer processionally object-torn is micro-regnant   a kindred non-appointment but due its least   a whole penalty (of person) missed before fir, preset only to praising intrinsic elongation through the mass it is   not every destitution is a gift unless in poverty for   counter-slightened taken in whole grain barren until or if only fir

on behalf of not being
the scale of prayer

as semi-equivalence
corrected *to* needle

prefacing nature with
silence perhaps but
waiting on a length of
branch pitched for
vocality at bay

Exercise the gulf of prayer in the drops of its unavoidances   fir makes common trench of the filters of this diversion   initial aporias are offered their throng: no steerage but this *is* cluster by prayer   gather the nearness things cannot bear, their own meaning is unshareable—until lifted onto our own conditions of a lesser upgradable, does encroach

questions sit to multiples
enough until
trashed overts:
let prayer open them
a prohesive openness

Prior provocation given its curt assemblies in unquaranteened fir   the encounter voids into tipped meaning: this contiguity for a neck-offered attendance we find pristine fir and do not instead encounter a whole degree of tremulous strain, the mark-out all listening done with as is non-locally completable spined of with we fall short of any possible switch from the blank frame of cry shortness of breath reverses the girth of tall tree in whose tenderness of link beseech

co-earthing which
desponds away from
increscence but onto
a sky's saturation
at the tails of fir

this precession to a sharp
shawl over being

two germs (prayer
towards, fir overhead)
instruct the one
excess

If origin doesn't return it includes the bulk plantation by which it doesn't repeat, non-iterant in crass occupation of ascent how fir cannot straggle or lag behind bands of prayer at a standing lost range but in breadth of no visible demotion fir as driven obstacles do converge on their trim in limbs that work prayer to its shift a scarcity caring of its distinct bifocal allocation because it brings in spares to the indifferent rubble double-closeting around each tree-base

no shelter outside
the intimacy of placing
prayer at the alteration

initial stint made plain
at: sharpness tries
the firs, its trans-
ferable (coated) diminution

out of oneself onto
a revealed bract of trees
not promptly beginning

If contingency sets the conditions it is a whole ontology's excess attrition   with indwelling attachments which meet the conditions of fir as additive horizon: a spark fletched amid perforated trees in recess of their gaps   as unsealed may straggle a path of violation but these micro-barbs are a shelter-scar giving the openness its sustaining overheads

not sub-rations of
finitude but a fir rebound
off ultra-compounds

a boundary not sur-
passed but consecutively
grown over

this retreat from source
to stalk carries an enig-
matic stringing of ground
a plantation's amount
of bundled steep

VII

The huddle of needle is sustained hindrance (vertical duress)   but given a latitude slimmer than entanglement in fir   firs are not simply, but an arc to their staying put with offcuts of prayer   nature can't propose a spire itself but only what it harbours when it does: that shelterable gust is not a dimension of the retreat itself   scarcely finding gift in its naked condition, no fir will shun the coatings of a perfectly adjunct penetration

amply driven
    onto the conjoinment
    a scarcity cone
    thrifty with overload

against any sufficiency
    of multiple form,
    offered a greater
    (leaner) range of
    draping the para-local

Gift beyond disposability but with a fellow opacity trans-generically reposing: how a shadow of the vertical is itself the only bridge-position in play   transcendence is downward so it is only prayer that abuts—across a fold of firs all spire to it   a further-than invites no surpassing but thickly waits at perpendicular girths, an under-tree which has its own unabandoned diminutions

how unstealthy giving
    might conceal
    companions in the given

apparent lessness to ground
    by which scarcity
    is combinatory
    the non-frugality
    of satisfied fir

Origin out-manoeuvred but creation's bleak exposure glazes the over-determination   rubs into the provisionality of things which hands on (the prayer position) a resistance only a next density amenably rare enough   a shard of vertical re-exposure but only after due attenuation in the sheltering obstacle   this is industrial seeding back-to-back on a sparser entail: if a nothing is *given* its lack, it will exceed nothing given: nothings pristine in fir lacking their own giftlessness   a lessness *in* gift lent onwards to prayer

concurrent breath through
        imposed fir generates
        condensed horizon
        rather than
        blows to locality

the erect hunger
        in everything
        prayable at post
        implicit, impliant

don't think the
        tapering in fir
        is unicellular:
        it has its confinities
        of reproductive slightness

Something still not cryable in this soil   that firs won't trust their spires to it   they do, however, invoke the stalemate of prayer   any sung throng might be a freshening-towards if firs were ever stockpiled: they would curtain the air, not spend prayer on safeguards   no such intimation without intimidation stalking the safety, towering the entrapment   fir signals are not so singular but squander well like prayer

a nearby virgin stand
        crammed green, the
        micro-quiver
        indexes full fir

unshorn by any
deals of placement

the prayer equally
unbiting, a-
symmetrically invited

leanest self-reckoning but
doesn't famish the opacity:
simply lay it beside the
redundant sentience
of blind-green firs

because there are
no such aisles
in prayer

www.ingramcontent.com/pod-product-compliance
Lightning Source LLC
Chambersburg PA
CBHW022009160426
43197CB00007B/354
9781848613843